*Praise for the true crime writing of*

JOHN STARK BELLAMY II

"Morbidly fascinating and wickedly entertaining . . . John Stark Bellamy II is the historian your mother warned you about . . . he offers bad guys and wanton women, unspeakable tragedy and murder most foul."
—*The Plain Dealer*

"Bellamy . . . [is a] Homer of our homicides, wandering through dark places and remembering." —*Free Times*

"[Bellamy's books] relate, in detail, the reasons, methods, and repercussions of a couple of centuries' worth of grisly acts. You'd have a tough time finding somebody in town more learned—or enthusiastic—about the city's history of death and disaster." —*Scene Magazine*

"Blood and tears drip from the pages." —*Akron Beacon Journal*

"Bellamy writes with razor-edged wit and his own particular brand of charm." —*Medina County Gazette*

"Bellamy writes his stories with the sensibility of a late 18th century reporter . . . Certainly, he chooses to write about crimes, but what emerges between the lines are stories of human suffering, stories of class struggle, stories that speak as much to the criminal mind as to the crime itself. And Bellamy clearly relishes his criminals. Sometimes he pokes fun. Sometimes he wonders at the humanity of it all. But always he tells his tales with sympathy, compassion and a good old-fashioned, if not antiquated, flair for storytelling." —*Sun Newspapers*

"Bellamy's way with words turns history into a current event."
—*Ohio Magazine*

"Bellamy blends details culled from old newspaper clippings, trial transcripts and other sources into an exploration of the city's seamier side."
—*West Life*

"Colorful and richly detailed writing." —*Chronicle Telegram*

"Bellamy's morbid subject matter, vividly drawn characters and flowery prose are reminiscent of Victorian murder mysteries, although the subjects hit closer to home." —*Maple Heights Press*

Also by John Stark Bellamy II:

*They Died Crawling*
*The Maniac in the Bushes*
*The Corpse in the Cellar*
*The Killer in the Attic*
*Death Ride at Euclid Beach*
*Women Behaving Badly (anthology)*

# CLEVELAND'S GREATEST DISASTERS!

## 16 TRAGIC TRUE TALES OF DEATH AND DESTRUCTION

**— an Anthology —**

JOHN STARK BELLAMY II

GRAY & COMPANY, PUBLISHERS
CLEVELAND

*With all my love to my beautiful wife, Laura,*
*the heroine of my disaster*

© 2009 by John Stark Bellamy II

All rights reserved. No part of this book may be reproduced or transmitted in any form or manner without written permission from the publisher.

The stories in this anthology originally appeared in the following books by John Stark Bellamy II, published by Gray & Company, Publishers: *They Died Crawling, The Killer in the Attic, The Corpse in the Cellar, The Maniac in the Bushes*, and *Death Ride at Euclid Beach.*

Photo credits appear on page 222.

Speaking engagements and narrative slide shows of many of these disasters are available from the author, who can be reached for such queries and any other purposes at his e-mail address: jstarkbi@tops-tele.com.

Gray & Company, Publishers
www.grayco.com

ISBN 978-1-59851-058-4

1.2

# CONTENTS

# PREFACE

It's hard to believe now, but disasters were my first love. True, the published evidence of the last 15 years belies the assertion—about 125 Cleveland crime stories against a mere score or so of Forest City catastrophes. But it's true—I virtually imbibed a taste for disasters with my mother's milk—and the first, fine, careless rapture of my late-blooming literary compulsion was to chronicle one of Cleveland's most memorable mishaps, rather than its murderous misdeeds.

That first venture was the story of the 1908 S. S. Kresge fireworks explosion, and it was in telling that tale that I began to learn the hard craft of describing such untoward events in persuasive and elucidatory detail. And it *was* hard, at least for me. For starters, I had read very few such accounts in my life, and I had no convenient model for the sort of brief, intensely local chronicle I had in mind. (To be precise, the only disaster accounts I had ever read were Robert Lansing's *Endurance,* his indelible account of Shackleton's terrifying expedition to the South Pole, and two books by Walter Lord: *A Night to Remember,* his celebrated narrative of the sinking of the *Titanic,* and his fine, if shorter history of the 1906 San Francisco earthquake, a chapter in his somewhat ironically titled best seller, *The Good Years.* Such wonderful and best-selling page-turners as *Isaac's Storm, The Perfect Storm,* and Stewart O'Nan's *The Circus Fire* were yet to come when I took my first stumbling steps into the realm of Cleveland woe.)

The other problem in devising such stories, I quickly learned, was simple to define, but difficult to solve. It was the vexing challenge that the key moments and events of a disaster usually come fast and furious, often happening almost or even simultaneously. The problem for the writer, then, is that he must capture and relate such closely occurring events in the clunky, linear form of words and sentences. Owing, no doubt, to my incompetence and experience, I had a lot of initial difficulty with this compositional conflict: I well remember the long days when, employing a scissors, I would carefully cut out each factoid, quote, and observation from the endless pages of my research notes of a disaster and paste them on large boards, painstakingly arranged so that the facts and relevant quotes of simultaneous events were horizontally accessible. Ironically enough, by the time I had finished this cumbersome assemblage, my brain was so saturated with every known fact that I was able to write the story practically off the top of my head without notes.

As mentioned, I developed an appetite for tales of woe very early in life. Part of this appetite was simply personal heritage. My grandfather Paul, a long-time Cleveland journalist and *Plain Dealer* editor-in-chief, often wrote about criminous and woeful matters. His first byline for the *Plain Dealer* in 1908 was an account of an old Ohio murder, and one of his last major efforts was a record of his 1946 tour of smithereened Germany, "A Trip Through Hell."

Less remotely, my father Peter was a career journalist for nearly half a century and my mother had served a grueling but colorful reportorial tutelage during the Depression as a Hearst reporter for the *Wisconsin News* in Milwaukee. Both my parents had seen some awful things, and, like most journalists, were not reticent in talking about them, often even in the presence of curious and impressionable children. Fifty-some years on, I can still recall my father's shock at the incredible devastation he had witnessed at the scene of the 1944 East Ohio Gas Company explosion and the terror aroused in Clevelanders by the devastation wrought by the 1954 West Side tornado. (Amble around Franklin Circle some time and discover why so much of this once-bijou residential junction is now devoid of such structures.)

Credit, too, should be awarded to my siblings for my precocious preoccupation with violent events. The first song I remember learning by heart (well, the first after *Heart and Soul,* that ubiquitous ditty heard in any 1950s household having a parlor piano and a child) was *The Ship Titanic,* courtesy of my sister Sheila, who had probably heard the song at C.Y.O. summer camp. (Discerning scholars of my works will recall that C.Y.O. camp as the place where I was first exposed to the delights of a good murder story, a demented counselor's tale of the hair-raising saga of "Mad Dog" Cahill.) It also in the verses of *The Ship Titanic* where I was first exposed to the inequitable realities of class conflict and their existential repercussions, factors which would loom large in my adult stories chronicling what happened to Clevelanders who could not afford to live, labor, or travel far enough away from perilous industrial and technological practices and dangers:

Oh, the ship was far from England
And headed for the shore,
When the rich refused to associate with the poor.
So they put the poor below
Where they'd be the first to go.
It was sad when the old grey ship sent down.

Ultimately, what I discovered in my research of Cleveland disasters was that such seemingly random and unpredictable mishaps in fact constituted a sort of unwritten biography of the city. And, as most of Cleveland's citizens throughout its history have been working class, I came to understand that almost all of my disaster narratives were object lessons of how the circumstances of Cleveland's socioeconomic arrangements guaranteed that they—not the middle or upper classes—would be the ones to bear the brunt of death and injury in any major disaster. Thus, it was largely the working-class muckers and sandhogs who were blown to pieces in all of the many waterworks tunnel construction disasters, not the white-collar administrators and public officials who were conveniently exonerated from blame at the ensuing inquests. And it was mainly ill-paid, socially negligible shop girls who perished in the 1908 S. S. Kresge fireworks holocaust, not the dime store owners and managers who encouraged the display, demonstration, and sale of lethal products. Ditto for Patrick Cleary and Patrick Toolis, the two workmen buried alive—but not for long—at the 103-foot bottom of one of the excavation pits for the Terminal Tower. Ditto for the victims of the 1949 National Air Races crash, the dead and injured of the 1902–1903 fireworks factory horrors, and virtually every victim of the almost innumerable streetcar and train accident fatalities which so decorated Cleveland outdoor life for nearly a century; it being no coincidence, as the Marxists used to say, that all rail tracks ran exclusively through working-class neighborhoods. Our ancestors had good reason to use the expression, "the wrong side of the tracks," and the record of Cleveland rail mishaps more than bears out the grim truth of the expression. True, the Cleveland Clinic and East Ohio Gas Company tragedies were partial exceptions to the rule, both yielding an impressive toll of well-to-do, or at least arguably middle-class victims. But it was no mistake or oversight that the lethal gas tanks happened to be situated in an ethnic, working-class neighborhood, instead of Bratenahl or even Cleveland Heights, and the so-called investigation of the Cleveland Clinic disaster was a paradigm of dismissive whitewashing that Pontius Pilate would have envied.

Returning to family influences, tribute should be paid to my brother Stephen, who indoctrinated me at a tender age in the fine art of chasing fire engines, a boyhood ritual which frequently interrupted family meals. A debt of gratitude is also owed to Denis Wood, who introduced me as an adolescent to the visual treasures of Lake View Cemetery, a holy grail for the morbidly historical mind. It was there, viewing its sobering memorial monument by the Euclid Avenue entrance, that I received my first hint of the almost unspeakable Collinwood school disaster. It was there, too, that I eventually found the grave of Garrett Morgan, the too-long-unsung hero of the waterworks tunnel blast, yet another reminder that the credit and the blame for Cleveland disasters are not generally distributed with any equity.

It is only fair to state, however, that the record of Cleveland's signature disasters, however horrific, could easily be duplicated in almost any great American city with a large population. (Conversely, regions lacking big cities are poor research grounds for the would-be disaster storyteller, as I found out after moving to Vermont, where *no* disasters of say, Cleveland caliber, have *ever* occurred.)Virtually all of our great metropolitan areas once possessed the conditions that made Cleveland's worst public tragedies possible: a rapidly expanding under class that provided an elastic labor pool unprotected from harm by law, regulation, or financial consequence to the employer; indifference in the governing elite and middle-class voters to the likely consequences of allowing dangerous manufacturing or industrial activities (*e.g.*, fireworks production or storage of liquefied natural gas) in lower-class residential areas; and the invariable siting of all rail lines, especially streetcar lines, in densely populated, less-prosperous neighborhoods. All of these conditions prevailed in large American cities during the late nineteenth and early twentieth centuries, and such realities, in Cleveland and elsewhere, added up to one simple truth for their inevitable victims: *They were expendable.* So let that be both the moral and motto for this collection of my favorite disaster stories.

Now, you might well ask why I am so fond of such tales, if their content is so grim and their moral so grave? Well, the simple truth is that I am enamored of the other side of the coin revealed in the telling of these Cleveland disasters. In virtually every one of these catastrophes, heroes and heroines, often to their own surprise, rose to the occasion on the spur of the moment and fearlessly risked their lives to save others imperiled, both loved ones and utter strangers. So it was that an obscure S. S. Kresge janitor, African-American Luther Roberts, repeatedly braved the flames and smoke of the exploding fireworks to drag helpless shop girls and shoppers to safety outside on a July day in 1908. So it was that 16-year-old Marcella Reichard of Lake Court stared through her window one October afternoon in 1944 to find the grass *and the pavement* burning from natural gas spewed from the exploded East Ohio Gas Company tanks across the street. Did she panic and think only of her own skin? No—she grabbed her mother and sister and led them to rescue through walls of flame and heat, in spite of her own serious burns. And so, too, acted the anonymous "Jimmy," a still-unidentified hero who looked at the blazing Cleveland Clinic one morning in May 1929 and said to a bystander, "That looks like gas; I'm going in there." Making at least two trips into that hospital inferno, he brought out several victims alive before simply disappearing back into obscurity. These, and the many other kindred heroes you will encounter in these 16 chapters, are Clevelanders worth celebrating, and in a just world would be remembered long after the Rockefellers, Wades, and other "famous" Clevelanders are forgotten. (Returning momentarily to the question of class inequity, it is a matter of record that most of Cleveland's "old money" denizens long ago deserted the city that made them and their progeny rich. But I digress.)

Readers of these pages may not be astonished to learn that as a child I loved comic books, especially those featuring superheroes such as Superman, Batman, and, my personal favorite, Sgt. Rock. As these tales of Cleveland woe bear witness, I still worship superheroes, and I like to think that I have found real ones in these narratives of the Cleveland past.

Let me say a word here about my principles of selection. Scale is obviously an important criterion in deciding which Cleveland catastrophes are worth chronicling. No Cleveland disaster book could sensibly exclude such lethal tragedies as the Collinwood school fire (175 dead), the East Ohio Gas explosion (130 dead), the Cleveland Clinic blast (128 dead), and the Ashtabula train wreck (perhaps 90 dead). But once the numbers are scaled down to a handful per episode, it becomes trickier to decide what is interesting and entertaining enough to justify the effort required both for the labor of the telling and the pains taken to read it.

Humor, if not quite ruled out, must be carefully rationed; most disasters have their funny (or at least "funny-peculiar") moments, but one has to be judicious in their inclusion and mindful of their effect on the necessarily somber tone of the story. For example, consider a story from the year 1878. On May 28, three men working in a privy on Grove Street were "overcome by fumes" and drowned. Now, privies may be funny, but drowning is considerably less amusing, so such a story ends up being more a candidate for Lanigan and Malone's "Knuckleheads in the News—The Historical Version" than a suitable chronicle of Cleveland woe. Ditto for the tale of William Nugent, who spent part of December 18, 1901 looking for a gas leak in his home at 1495 Lorain Street. His method of search involved lighting matches, which eventually triggered an explosion that blew him through a window into the street, wrecked his home, and injured five other persons. And how about the unidentified chump who, while attempting to kill a cockroach with gasoline, set the Caxton Building afire in 1908? Or the Pentecostal Speaking in Tongues congregation, whose July 17, 1908 meeting at East 49th and Cedar Avenue was disrupted by someone throwing a mass of limburger cheese into the midst of the worshipers, sparking a panic that led to several members being badly trampled? Or poor Richard Cusimano, who crashed a truck carrying 7,600 pounds of marijuana on Interstate 90 in 1982, which resulted in prison for him and the marijuana being burned in a Republic Steel furnace? Or—my personal favorite—the crash of a P. O. C. beer truck on the Main Avenue Bridge on September 23, 1954. The overturned truck, which tied up rush-hour traffic for hours, also spewed beer from its ruptured tanks for some time on grateful Clevelanders below. All worthy stories in some sense, to be sure, but a little too flippant in the company of such heartbreakers as the Collinwood school horror and the waterworks tunnel inferno. (For the record: the only Cleveland woe story which has ever caused me personal anguish or any psychic discomfort is the Collinwood school fire story. Back in the late '90s, I spent several months compiling a slide show and, after living for several months with pathetic visual images of the dead children, I began to feel positively haunted.)

But rest assured: buried deep in the Bellamy archives is an encyclopedic calendar of over 15,000 incidents of Cleveland woe, the fruit of my two decades of researching and indexing virtually every bad thing that has ever happened in Cleveland. Someday *all* of Cleveland's woe may yet be told . . . but in the meantime, I have chosen to focus on those stories with the highest quotient of personality, poignancy, and heroism.

Compared to my more voluminous murder stories, my literary debts in the composition of these Cleveland disaster stories are slight. But I could not have even written my first disaster story without the inspiration of George Condon, the all-time dean of Cleveland writers and the man who proved that one could bring not only scholarship, but also humor and a beguiling style to the writing of Cleveland history.

Another role model for being a Cleveland writer was Peter Jedick, whose example of careful research and zest for all things Cleveland kept me going forward when my path was unclear.

Thanks are also due to William Barrow and his staff in the *Cleveland Press* collection at the Cleveland State University library. Their pictorial treasures and astute counsel were indispensable resources during my 20-year pilgrimage through the annals of Cleveland woe.

I also wish to thank the staff at the Fairview Park Regional Branch of the Cuyahoga County Public Library, especially Jennifer Gerrity, Rebecca Groves, and the late Marty Essen, who tirelessly and patiently expedited my periodical researches and calmly tolerated my odious pencil-chewing habit. Profound thanks are due to librarian Avril McInally of the same institution, who provided much support and encouragement during my writing years and even once, at my earnest behest, spent the soggy Halloween night of 1994 crawling, in company with my daughter Sarah, around the turf of the Monroe Street Cemetery, vainly seeking the grave of 18-year-old Erma Schumacher, a victim of the S. S. Kresge tragedy. (Alas, I never discovered Erma's final resting place; the cemetery records are sketchy, but it appears that her remains were transferred to another site some years after her death.)

And I will never forget the gratitude owed to *Plain Dealer* writer Evelyn Theiss, whose early championship of my work and kindred enthusiasm for Cleveland woe remain among the highest rewards enjoyed during my lengthy toil on the dark and bloody ground of Cleveland history.

# CLEVELAND'S GREATEST
# DISASTERS!

# STREETS OF HELL

## The East Ohio Gas Company Explosion and Fire

## (1944)

It happens very suddenly, as you drive north through the neighborhood straddling St. Clair Avenue near East 55th Street on Cleveland's northeast side. Where residential housing still persists in the upper 50s, there are mostly modest frame dwellings of turn-of-the-century vintage—small houses on postage-stamp lots, so crammed together as to give passersby claustrophobia just looking between them. Unless you know the dire history of this place, however, you aren't prepared for the abrupt architectural change that begins north of St. Clair on East 63rd Street and persists westward to East 55th. Little by little, and then suddenly, the frame houses disappear and in their stead one finds modest, brick dwellings of a post–World War II character. And the closer you get to the property of the East Ohio Gas Company, the more modern brick homes you find—until residential housing ceases completely at the peaceful green border of Grdina Park, today the southern perimeter of the once-enormous gas company grounds. There's a reason for that park, and there's a reason for that eruption of modern, brick homes. For this is the Norwood–St. Clair neighborhood, once and still the heart of Cleveland's Slovene community and the site of Cleveland's worst industrial disaster: The East Ohio Gas Company Explosion and Fire of 1944.

How bad was it? Well, in terms of the bald body count, it wasn't the worst Cleveland area disaster: at 130 known dead it barely surpassed the Cleveland Clinic Fire of 1929—by a mere five corpses—and fell more than 40 short of the 1908 Collinwood School Fire death toll. But for sheer horror, its effect on a large community, and the physical destruction involved it would be hard to beat. Of its 130 dead, 61 were so badly burned or pulverized that identification, sometimes even as to the sex of the corpse, proved impossible. Seventy-three of the dead were employees of East Ohio Gas. The disaster injured 225 persons badly enough to require hospital treatment, 23 of them Cleveland firemen. It totally destroyed 79 houses, 2 factories, 217 automobiles, 7 trailers, and 1 tractor, and partially destroyed another 35 houses and 13 factories. It did extensive damage not only to the Gas Company #2 works but also to property or facilities owned by Bell Telephone, the Cleveland Transit System, the New York Central Railroad, the Pennsylvania Railroad, and Western Union. The total damage amounted to between $6 million and $8 million. Not to mention the cost of repairing the surrounding streets and sewer systems, largely smithereened into a splintered landscape of cavernous craters, and the promiscuous wreckage of subsidiary gas explosions.

Dollars, of course, don't tell the real story. The explosion and fire that turned most of East 61st, 62nd, 63rd, Lake Court, and Carry Avenue into neighborhood holocausts burnt out the heart of a deeply rooted, cohesive, supportive, ethnic community. That community would proudly recover and rebuild—but no one involved could ever pretend that things would be the same.

Again, how bad was it? It was the force of 130 billion British Thermal Units (BTUs) unleashed within 30 minutes on a mere 160-acre area, much of it congested residential housing. It was 25 millions of horsepower suddenly vented to destroy hundreds of homes, families, and lives. It was searing, scorching flames, reaching heights of 2,800 feet and 3,000 degrees Fahrenheit in streets where children played and retirees sat on their front porches of a sunny October afternoon. It comprised the destructive force con-

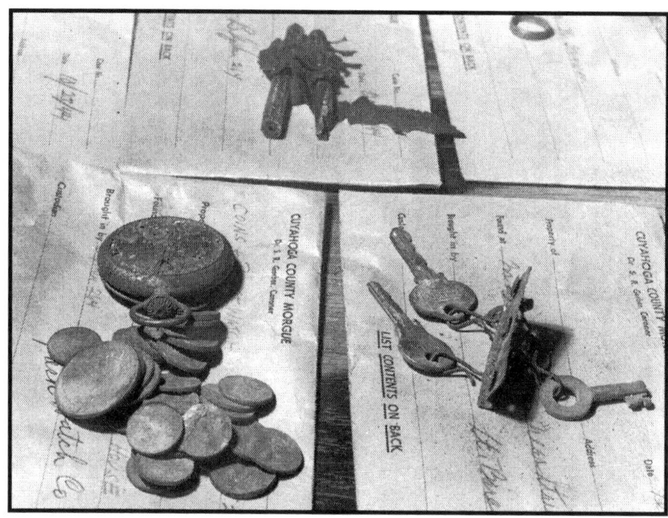


Melted coins and keys from unidentified victims of the East Ohio Gas Company Fire.

tained in 10,000 tons of coal or, say, the energy of 120 minutes' worth of all the hydroelectric power west of the Mississippi devoted to the cause of blowing up and burning down the Norwood–St. Clair community.

After it was over, everyone agreed—*surprise!*—that it *never* should have happened. East Ohio Gas Company officials argued, quite correctly, that the explosion should not have occurred, given the laws of probability and the precautions taken to prevent it. City and neighborhood leaders excoriated both the gas company and city fathers for allowing such a lethal facility to be built so near a residential neighborhood. The fact of the matter is that the East Ohio Gas Company fire came, like Carl Sandburg's fog, on little cat feet. Decisions, both residential and industrial, unwittingly taken over decades of development, quietly and steadily made it almost inevitable that the East Ohio tragedy would happen just the way it did. All it took was a dangerous facility located close to a fragile, congested neighborhood. The East Ohio Gas Company #2 plant, located cheek-by-jowl to the Slovenian neighborhood of the East

60s, provided just such a site . . . and the exigencies of World War II energy production and distribution ensured that the disaster would occur in a certain way in that very particular place at that precise time.

The East Ohio Gas Company works located north of St. Clair and east of East 55th (formerly Willson Avenue) was one of the oldest industrial sites in Cleveland. Developed originally by the Cleveland Gas Light & Coke Company in the mid-19th century, the gas works became a part of the extensive East Ohio Gas Company properties shortly after the turn of the century. Known eventually as the #2 works, the 10-acre gas company grounds east of East 55th and north of St. Clair became a major nexus for the storage and distribution of natural gas to East Ohio's many thousands of customers throughout Ohio. Meanwhile, just to the south of the #2 works, a vigorous ethnic neighborhood was developing simultaneously, and with little coordination to its industrial northern neighbor. Most of the housing stock was built between 1895 and 1905, predominately modest, working-class houses on very narrow, short lots, many of them two- or even four-family homes. This predominately Slovenian community stretched along the axis of St. Clair Avenue from the East 30s well into the East 70s, with the emotional focus of the community centering on St. Vitus Church, a Catholic nationality parish created in 1893.

It was only in the 1940s that the character of the #2 works changed in a manner threatening to the actual existence of the neighborhood. Owing to fluctuations in the rate of supply and limited storage capacity, East Ohio Gas was having trouble meeting the needs of its customers, especially during times of peak demand, such as prolonged winter cold spells. Supply problems were further aggravated by the war, and gas service to East Ohio customers had to be curtailed a number of times in the early 1940s. Something had to be done, and the solution chosen was a gas liquefication-regasification facility. And it was to be located at the heart of the utility's service area, the center of Cleveland's East Side.

The technology of natural gas liquefication had been under development for a half century, with most of the technical advances made by German chemists. The scientific concept was simple and its practical advantages were obvious: transformation of natural gas to a liquid state at minus 260 degrees Fahrenheit involves a volume reduction ratio of 640:1. To be able to store 640 times as much natural gas as could be stored in its gaseous state, for regasification and use at peak demand times, was an irresistible option for East Ohio Gas, and they exercised it by constructing three liquid storage units of spherical design.

Built at a cost of $1.5 million, the three tanks were completed in January 1941. Their total capacity was 150,000,000 cubic feet. An adjoining regasification plant could convert the liquid back to gas at a rate of 3,000,000 cubic feet per hour. Storage commenced on February 7, 1942, and the plant quickly proved its commercial worth. But there were still shortages as wartime production demands increased, so East Ohio Gas Company received permission from the War Production Board on August 3, 1942 to build a fourth tank of 100,000,000 cubic feet capacity, double the size of its existing #1, #2, and #3 tanks.

There were some critical differences in the design of the fourth tank. Unlike the first three tanks, it was of cylindrical design. The first three tanks, in fact, were designed as spheres-within-spheres, the inner gas-holding sphere being insulated from its outer containing sphere by cork, with the entire 57-foot-high structure supported and suspended by steel supports. The fourth tank was a cylinder-within-a-cylinder (technically called a toro-segmental two-cylinder) and its inner insulation between the cylinders was composed of rock wool. The contrasting designs reflected, mainly, wartime economies. Despite its higher capacity, the #4 cylinder tank used 100 fewer tons of steel than a comparable spherical design, in part because it required fewer steel supports. Since cork was a critical war materiel, rock wool was chosen as the substitute insulation. As was the case with the other tanks, the inner gas-holding shell of the 50-foot-high #4 was constructed using a three-and-a-half-percent nickel-steel alloy to construct.

Designed and built by the Pittsburgh–Des Moines Steel Company, the #4 tank went into service in March 1943. But not for long. While being filled for the first time, the bottom of the inner steel shell cracked because of uneven cooling, and it had to be rebuilt. It was soon back in service, although it seems that the cooling problem was not corrected. Neighborhood air-raid wardens would complain periodically over the next year and a half that there was frequent "frosting" on the surface of the tank, obviously caused by settling of the rock wool insulation, which allowed outside moisture to settle on relatively uninsulated spots between the inner and outer shells of the #4 tank.

Friday, October 20, 1944, arrived and waxed as a beautiful, crisp fall day in Cleveland. Things were humming at the #2 works. In anticipation of the coming winter, the L.S.&R. crew of 24 was topping off the last of the four tanks, #1, and expected to finish the job about 2 p.m. As that hour came, no one, later, remembered anything unusual. East Ohio Gas Company Assistant Chief Engineer John R. Feightner and Engineer Hugh O'Donnel were underneath the #4 tank searching for a steam hose about 2:15, and noticed nothing out of the ordinary. Mrs. Charles Flickinger, 36, of 5614 Carry Avenue, was cleaning house and was just about to plug in her sweeper. Mrs. Thomas Komor, also of Carry Avenue, was walking with her two-year-old daughter, Judy, to a grocery store on E. 61st Street. Mrs. Julia Torok, 44, of 1162 E. 58th Street, was on her way to her husband's barbershop on the south side of St. Clair at East 55th Street. And Marcella Reichard, 16, of 5473 Lake Court, was mopping the kitchen floor. Most school-age neighborhood children were in classes at Willson Elementary School on East 55th, anticipating the end of the school day and their return home in 20 minutes. The sun was shining and the wind was between 10 and 16 miles per hour. The time was 2:40 p.m.

No one will ever know with certainty just why and how the #4 cylindrical tank blew up at that moment. Most of the witnesses close to the initial disaster were killed, most of them the very East Ohio Gas Company technicians whose expertise might have most aided

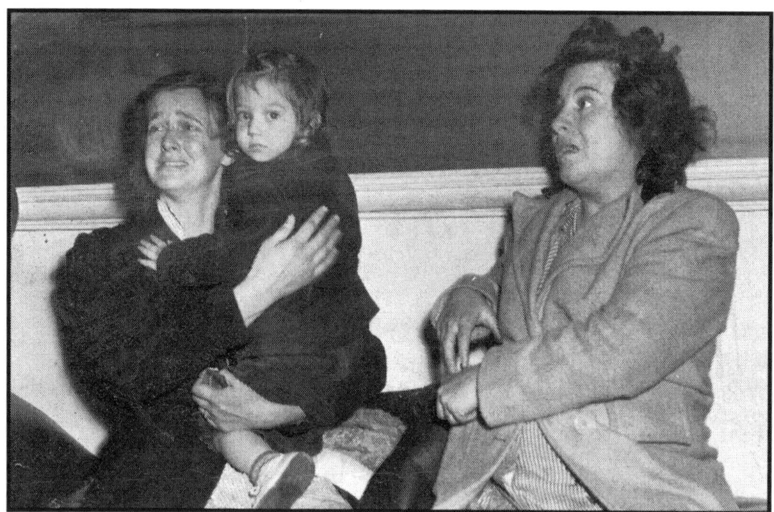

Distraught relatives, Willson School, Oct. 20, 1944. Mrs. Janice Komar, Judy Komar and Mrs. Charles Flickinger.

the ensuing investigations. But various witnesses in scattered locations later reported "heavy, white, steam-like vapors creeping and rolling" in the #4 vicinity about 2:30 p.m. Some of them thought the leak started about 10 feet off the ground and went halfway up the #4 tank. Two expert witnesses saw the blast preliminaries. H. J. Hense, of the American Gas Association Laboratories on East 55th, across the street from the liquid gas tanks, looked out the window about that time and noticed a leak in #4, with snow-white vapor or liquid gas streaming out. Seconds later he saw a second stream. John R. Feightner, the chief engineer of the L.S.& R plant, reacted immediately to what he saw. Standing in the center north door of the gas compressor building, he spied the cloud of white vapor and said, even as he began to run for his life, "My God, Number Four has let go!"

The first explosion came at about 2:41 p.m. The billowing clouds streaming out from #4 were suddenly illuminated at various points by rapid, yellowish-orange flashes. Seconds later came a tremendous blast, which shook the ground as far away as Shaker

Square, and the flames of which were seen in Chagrin Falls. Almost instantaneously, a good deal of the 29-acre area including and surrounding the #2 works was on fire.

Outside the immediate blast area, waves of heat began to blow southward. Automobiles travelling on East 55th had their tires suddenly blown out from the heat radiating through the asphalt, and workers at the Warner & Swasey plant all the way down on Carnegie Avenue had to shut their windows against the intense heat. Meanwhile, young reporter George Condon was talking to the men's fashion editor on the 6th floor of the *Plain Dealer* building when, suddenly, over the editor's shoulder, he saw an immense pillar of flame rising on the northeastern skyline. He and his fellow reporters immediately left the building, heading east.

The first alarm was pulled at 2:41 p.m., and by the time the first Cleveland Fire Department company arrived at 2:43 many of the houses on East 61st and East 62nd were burning like torches. Fire officials and other witnesses later reported that many of the houses closest to the #4 tank at the northern end of East 61st seemed to be burning from the inside out. The reason for this soon became horrifyingly clear. Apparently in the minutes between the initial gas leak and the first explosion, a lot of liquid gas had seeped into the sewer system in the St. Clair area. Thousands of gallons of liquid fuel had already penetrated residential plumbing and drainage systems when ignition came, and shocked eyewitnesses watched as streams of flame raced up and down the neighborhood streets from catch basin to catch basin.

Aside from the force of the initial explosion, two factors increased the intensity of the initial inferno. One was the nature of the gas itself. As it was transformed back into its gaseous state by contact with the air, it became flammable, not to mention expanding to 640 times its liquid volume. Its presence in the sewer system and area house basements guaranteed that each home became an expanding holocaust as soon as ignited. The other factor was the unforeseen agency of the rock wool insulation, blown into countless liquid-gas-soaked fragments by the initial blast. Many of the rock wool pieces became flaming incendiaries that soon ignited numberless subsidiary fires.

Those who survived the first few minutes of the explosion and fires had terrible, touching stories to tell. One of them was Mrs. Berta Ott of 5472 Lake Court. As she later recalled:

> Out of my window I see everything all red right after I hear the big noise. When I open the door the grass was burning in the yard already. So hot was it I didn't know whether to open the door or not. All the children but Geraldine were at school. We ran out . . . We run through the field. All was burning. My back was so hot I thought I was myself on fire already. I took so good care of everything. My dog Tootsie—she was to have puppies—my three cats, my chicken all gone. My poor Tootsie.

Another woman with memories of instant hell was Mrs. Charles Flickinger of Carry Ave, the housewife who had just been about to plug in her carpet sweeper at 2:40 p.m.:

> Suddenly it seemed like the walls turned red. I looked at the windows and the shades were on fire. Just like that. The house filled up with smoke. I think the furnace had blown up. Then I go out and see the fire all around.

There were many heroes and heroines in the first few minutes after the #4 explosion. One was Jack Bogarty of 6357 St. Clair, who had no idea what was going on when the doors of his house suddenly blew in:

> I thought we had visitors. A second later we heard the explosion. A hot wave of air filled the house. I grabbed little Georgene off the couch and ran outside.

Bogarty's experience was typical of the dozens of residents who conquered their initial fear of a world on fire to concentrate on

Pumper #7 in crater, Norwood and St. Clair, Oct. 20, 1944.

helping others get to safety. Perhaps the most celebrated of this breed was Marcella Reichard, 16, of Lake Court. When the first blast knocked the mop out of her hand, she ran outside and saw that not only was the grass on fire but even the pavement, too. Marcella knew what to do, though:

> I grabbed my mother and my little sister and we knelt and prayed. Mother went out the back way, and I told her she would be running right into the flame. I told them to hold their hands over their eyes and run toward the lake. Then we just ran.

Marcella also tried to save an elderly next-door neighbor without success, not to mention a cache of letters from her soldier boyfriend overseas. She ended up badly burned all over her face and left arm, but she managed to save her family. She was also responsible for, perhaps, the most eloquently homely description of the disaster, "The whole kitchen looked as if the sun were setting right in the room."

The local residents weren't the only people with horrific stories to tell. Seventy-three of the 130 people who died that afternoon worked for the East Ohio Gas Company, and the surviving utility employees and those at neighboring businesses had terrible memories of what they saw as they fled the spreading holocaust. Within seconds of the #4 blast, virtually everything in the area was on fire: buildings, vehicles, utility wires, asphalt streets, grass, sewers, and a large number of human beings and animals. (In addition to dogs and cats, many area residents raised chickens; only the area cats had a high survival rate). Or as Mrs. Frank Mervar, of Mervar Cleaners at 5372 St. Clair, put it:

> Everywhere you looked, every little leaf, every twig branch, the telephone wires, everything was a mass of flames. I was sure we were being bombed.

A very lucky East Ohio employee was engineer John Feightner. He had already started running when the first blast knocked him off his feet, but he got up and managed to make it into the #9 Water Seal Holder, which was a water-well area within a nearby gas drainage container. Seconds later, Feightner saw fellow employee Dale Keller running by, enveloped in flames. He managed to get his attention, and Keller jumped into the well with him, extinguishing his flames. Meanwhile, another employee ran by in flames, but Feightner and Keller were unable to get him into the well. They watched until he stopped running, fell down, and burned to death. After some minutes in the well, Keller and Feightner got out and started running north toward Lake Erie. They had just gotten to the New York Central railroad tracks when the #3 tank exploded.

It isn't surprising that #3 blew up at 3 p.m., about 20 minutes after the first blast. Given the force of the #4 blast and the temperatures of up to 3,000 degrees Fahrenheit, it is surprising only that it took 20 minutes to melt the steel supports of #3 enough for it to collapse and detonate. More surprising still, however, was the fact that the #1 and #2 tanks *did not* blow up, despite their proximity to the two exploding tanks and the intense heat. For hours, virtually helpless firefighters watched and waited for #1 and #2 to blow . . . but it never happened.

Only the pen of a Dante could do justice to the sights and sounds that occurred in the St. Clair-Norwood neighborhood that hellish afternoon. Many of the human casualties were later found where they had died on the streets and in the houses adjacent to the #2 works. In the years to come there would be legends of completely cremated bodies found in the metal lockers of the East Ohio Gas Company Meter building, where terrified humans had locked themselves in to escape the heat—but such stories are apparently apocryphal. Thousands of birds, mostly sparrows, were instantly melted out of the sky and off telephone wires, as flames arced thousands of feet high, releasing temperatures usually not encountered outside a blast furnace. Meanwhile, the streets—East 55th, East 61st, East 62nd, East 63rd, St. Clair Avenue, Carry Avenue, and Lake Court—were littered with the pyres of burning human beings and the homes they had once inhabited.

As might be expected, the disaster did not bring out the best in everyone. Although initially Sea Scouts from local Coast Guard units and, eventually, the National Guard were put in place to prevent looting, not much could be done to defeat the ingenuity and ghoulish interest of many Clevelanders in the tragedy rapidly unfolding on the city's northeast side. There was a reported incident of children being trampled by a crowd of rubberneckers, who panicked when the wind suddenly shifted the flames toward them on East 55th. And there is a memorable photograph of crowds waiting for the trolley on Saturday, October 24, at Marquette and East 79th. Many of them repeatedly rode this line back and forth all day, as it afforded the best view of the otherwise sealed-off neighborhood.

The response of safety officials was rapid and well organized, but there was little they could initially do, except to rescue the rescuable and to seal off the neighborhood. Because of the release of liquid gas into the local sewer system, much of the water system was soon destroyed by a series of subsidiary explosions which continued to blow craters in the streets and pop manhole covers hundreds of feet high throughout the rest of the day. Many of the newspaper reporters who covered the catastrophe would remember the latter phenomenon best, especially their frenzied panic as exploding manhole covers chased them up and down the smoldering streets. *Cleveland Press* reporter William Dapo remembered:

> The exploding sewers for a time seemed worse than the fire itself. I was standing at Norwood Ave. and St. Clair when the blast so buckled the street a fire truck was buried in a huge crater. There was a hissing sound, then a roaring blast lifted the truck into the air. Flying bricks and glass flew all over the intersection. Too scared to run and too scared to lie down, I managed to move about three feet—to see beneath those feet another manhole cover. I took off then, but fast.

In practical terms the multiple sewer and street explosions meant that there was little water with which to fight fires that already encompassed an eight-block area. Thanks to the lakefront presence of the Coast Guard, however, a 1,500-foot hose was soon rigged up from a lake tug and water began to pour onto fires from the south side of the New York Central Railroad tracks. Meanwhile, the area from East 53rd east to Addison Road and south from Lake Erie to St. Clair was evacuated of more than 10,000 residents and sealed off.

The timing of the neighborhood quarantine was full of pathos, as it was accomplished just as neighborhood children were let out of Willson Elementary on East 55th. They arrived at the perimeter of their neighborhood to find it in flames—and probably their loved ones, too—and were sent back to Willson, where the Red Cross quickly established a disaster relief center. That night, 680 area residents slept on cots there, most still ignorant of the fate of their loved ones back in the burning inferno they had called home. Meanwhile, the County Morgue down on Lake Avenue at East 9th was besieged by a hysterical, weeping mob, desperate for news of missing relatives.

It is hard to say when the fire was brought "under control." Cleveland firemen claimed mastery about midnight (Saturday morning). Residents were allowed to return to most areas on Sunday morning, October 22, although some fires continued to smolder for days, and small, exploding pockets of gas continued to make life interesting for reporters and safety forces for some time after the flames had dissipated.

As in all disasters, there were some oddities that were never accounted for. Given the intensity of the blasts and the heat of the flames, a great number of homes on the streets nearest to the #2 works were completely destroyed, as even a casual drive down East 61st, East 62nd, or Carry Avenue makes manifest today. Homes many blocks away had paint blistered and stripped by the volcanic temperatures. Yet some homes relatively near the center of the disaster escaped damage almost entirely, and the same could be said for some lucky human beings, who inexplicably survived a catastrophe that killed most of their neighbors. Not to mention such freakish events as the death of Minnie Schwebs of 1011 East 61st St. Burned over her entire body, her clothes burnt off completely and her charred flesh hanging in grotesque shreds, Schwebs apparently walked from East 61st to Glenville Hospital, where she collapsed and died. Physicians could only conjecture that extreme shock kept her going long after she should have succumbed to her burns.

If forethought was lacking in the period leading up to the East Ohio Gas disaster, the aftermath certainly afforded careful hindsight and recrimination. After the flames were brought under control, some rather intrepid gas workers began to drain the liquid gas out of Tanks #1 and #2. This took several days, as there was no power available in the area and three locomotives had to be brought in on the New York Central tracks to provide power for the drainage operation. Meanwhile, Coroner Sam Gerber supervised the grisly task of searching for the many missing bodies and the accumulation and classification of evidence.

It was ghastly work, somewhat hampered by poor early-November weather and the unsafe condition of many of the damaged buildings which contained the bodies of the missing. Of 130 bodies

Aerial view of East Ohio disaster, Oct. 20, 1944.

in the official tally, 61 were so badly burned or pulverized that no identification could be made. Most of them, like the 69 corpses identified, were either neighborhood residents or gas company employees. But some of them were just unlucky souls who happened to be in the wrong place at the wrong time. People like Louis Ringhoff and Joseph Meidler, roofing contractors, who just happened to be repairing the roof of a #2 works building that Friday afternoon when they were instantly incinerated. Likewise, James A. Conforti, 23, of Cornell Road, survived the blast but suffered severe burns. It seems he was putting himself through chiropody school by giving driving lessons, and he had unluckily picked the Norwood–St. Clair area for his student's lesson that Friday afternoon. Conversely, there were lucky individuals like George P. Binder. Superintendent of the liquid gas units, Binder, 45, was out in the field when the disaster struck. Virtually everyone in the office where he usually worked was killed as he watched from afar in horror.

Many of the neighborhood residents had to cope with the loss of their life savings, in addition to losing their families and homes. Among the saddest sights of the disaster, observers remarked, were the many scenes of returned residents weeping over burnt tin boxes and cans. Like many Americans who had lived through the Depression, area residents were suspicious of banks, all the more so as a large neighborhood bank had failed during the 1930s. So when the fire came, it incinerated numerous boxes and lard tins of cash and war bonds that householders had stashed under their mattresses and in their basements. The bonds would be replaced eventually by the U.S. government but the currency was redeemable only if still largely intact. More complex financial problems were presented by the estates of victims whose wills had also been destroyed in the fire. Not to mention the difficulties of probating cash and silver found on the bodies of the dead.

East Ohio Gas Company, for its part, moved toward settlement of claims as rapidly as possible. It had good reason to do so, as hungry lawyers were already swarming like a Biblical plague on Norwood–St. Clair, hot on the heels of the vulnerable, returning residents. An office was quickly opened to process claims against the utility, and the company astutely sought to protect itself from bogus claims by conducting a thorough photographic inventory of every structure and vehicle in the affected neighborhood. This proved a prudent precaution, as in one case where a claimant came in with only a license plate, claiming all evidence of the vehicle it had belonged to had been destroyed in the fire.

By mid-November the search for the dead, conducted by 80 men with picks and shovels from the county engineer's department, was complete. More than half the casualties were represented only by bone fragments or body stumps. On November 14, 1944, a mass funeral and burial for the 61 unidentified dead was held in Highland Park Cemetery. There, before a crowd of 2,000, each body or body part was buried in a separate casket in an individual concrete vault. Each body received an individual grave number and the remains were carefully inventoried. Later, a simple, moving commemorative marker within a quiet garden was erected at the gravesite. All caskets, hearses, and the services of the funeral directors were donated.

Mass grave burial service for East Ohio Gas Company fire victims at Highland Park Cemetery, Nov.14, 1944.

And that was that, except for the rebuilding of the neighborhood—and the pleasures of the recriminations to come. Thanks to some insurance money, the eventual proceeds of almost 2,000 fire-loss claims filed against the gas company, and—above all—the efforts of the local Slovenian community itself, the neighborhood was rebuilt. The indomitable Slovenian residents would settle for nothing less. Mrs. Frances Skully, a 68-year-old widow, may well have spoken for the neighborhood as she returned to the ruins of her home at 1036 East 61st Street:

> I'd be willing to set up a cot in my chicken coop and go back again. I couldn't think of living anywhere else. I could go through the neighborhood blindfolded. I know every step of the way. All my friends are there; where else would I want to go?

In addition to its $3-million neighborhood settlements, the East Ohio Gas Company also paid more than a half-million dollars in settlements to the families of its injured and dead employees.

The nine separate investigations ensuing from the explosion and fire were less productive. The most ambitious probe was launched by Mayor Frank Lausche within 24 hours of the disaster. Lausche, who had grown up in the Norwood–St. Clair neighborhood, knew every inch and resident of the afflicted area, and he expected his appointed 12-man committee to produce some answers. Meanwhile, Coroner Gerber, never shy of publicity, launched his own probe, while the National Board of Fire Underwriters also sent a team to investigate.

The committees made heroic efforts to get to the bottom of the #4 blast, but the conclusions of the Lausche committee and its kindred bodies were neither very conclusive nor impressive, given the expectations placed on them. Virtually everyone agreed that the "location of the plant was poorly chosen in view of the surroundings and potential destructiveness of the stored liquid." In addition, the committees faulted the diking and drainage systems at the #2 works as inadequate. Gerber spoke for the future, if not, alas, for the past, when he concluded that no plant of the #2 type should be built in a "residential, semi-residential, business, or congested area." Apropos of this conclusion was a moment of probably unintended and undetected black humor, which came during the interrogation of a steel company official. When asked if he thought it would be a good idea to build any future L. S. & R. works so near a residential area, the official thoughtfully averred, "Well, just from a public-relations point of view, it would not be a very good idea."

None of the committees ever got to the bottom of the #4 failure.

Perhaps the one person who came out of the tragedy best was sly Sam Gerber, the perpetual county coroner of Cleveland in the mid-20th century. His rapid and assured handling of the mass autopsies and body search enhanced his already prominent political profile and *his* report astutely avoided conflict with a local utility giant by blaming . . . the Pittsburgh–Des Moines Steel Company, for overestimating the stability of its cylindrical design. Interestingly, no one ever seriously pursued the question of why area sewer lines—in contrast to standard practice—were not sealed to prevent the infiltration of gas.

East Ohio Gas Company shut down its remaining works at the #2 site soon after the disaster, and at the former site of the lethal tanks, Grdina Park stands today. The company still maintains its handsome office building on East 55th, just north and west of the fatal scene. All the residential streets were eventually reconstructed—except for that area taken up by Grdina Park and Lake Court where 27 houses burned to the ground. The latter street was abandoned as a residential area and today is given over completely to commercial and industrial use.

The last words, of course, belong to the victims, or at least to those with the most right to speak for them. Those words, somewhat ambiguous, are found on the plaque affixed to the monumental obelisk to the unknown dead of the explosion fire at Highland Park Cemetery:

> SOCIAL PROGRESS
> ATTUNED TO INDUS-
> TRIAL ACHIEVEMENTS
> FOR THE BENEFIT OF
> THE LIVING SHALL
> BE A MEMORIAL TO
> THESE WHOSE LIVES
> WERE UNWITTINGLY
> SACRIFICED
> OCT. 20, 1944

On the reverse of the monument is another plaque identifying the dead as those of the Norwood–St. Clair disaster. The East Ohio Gas Company is not even mentioned.

# "WE ARE GOING DOWN!"

## The Ashtabula Bridge Disaster (1876)

The world was a howling, smothering white wasteland that fateful night in Ashtabula. It was Friday, December 29, 1876, and for two days an intense winter blizzard had been pummeling the small country town, located in the northeast corner of Ohio, with up to 20 inches of snow and winds up to 55 miles an hour. Nevertheless, the town train depot was crowded and bustling that Christmas week evening, with some awaiting incoming trains and others about to depart. And the most anxious in the throng were those waiting for the No. 5 "Pacific Express," due in from Erie, Pennsylvania, on the Lake Shore & Michigan Southern railway. It was already two hours late, and the word was that it had not gotten out of Erie until after 6 p.m.

Things were more cheerful and relaxed on the No. 5 train. Drawn by two powerful locomotives pulling two express cars, two baggage cars, two passenger cars, one smoking car, and three sleeping cars, the No. 5 was chugging steadily through the white winter night at 10 miles an hour, its comfortable passengers oblivious to the frigid fury outside. Many of them were conversing or eating, some were playing cards, and yet others were nestled in their sleeping berths. Others prepared themselves for their imminent departure at Ashtabula or warmed themselves at the coal-fired Baker steam heaters that provided warmth to all cars except the smoker, which was furnished with an old-fashioned wood stove. No one afterwards could ever be sure, but there were at least 128 passengers and 19 crewmen aboard at 7:23 p.m. as the No. 5 roared onto the railway bridge spanning Ashtabula Creek.

Daniel McGuire, the engineer of the "Socrates," the lead locomotive, was the first to realize there was a problem. As he entered the bridge, he pulled the throttle out, increasing his train's speed to about 12 miles per hour, the acceleration needed to drive the train through the two feet of snow on the tracks and the stiff, gale-force winds. As the "Socrates" approached the western abutment of the 154-foot bridge, McGuire suddenly had the terrifying sensation that his engine was "running uphill." Turning his head, he looked back and gaped in horror as he saw the rest of his train—the second locomotive "Columbia" and the 11 cars—falling with the collapsing bridge toward the creek, 82 feet below. Almost simultaneously, McGuire pulled the throttle out again, giving the "Socrates" a surge of power that broke its coupling with the "Columbia" and pushed it the last critical 80 feet uphill to the western abutment and safety. As he hit the brakes on the other side, McGuire heard a frightful crashing noise behind and below.

William Asell, a telegraph operator, was the first person at the depot, only 1,000 feet east of the bridge, to realize what had happened. Hoping to hitch a ride through town with the train, he had heard the whistle of the No. 5 as it entered the bridge and was walking toward it to see whether it was a passenger or freight train. When he saw that it was a passenger train, he turned around and began walking back to the station. Seconds later, he heard a terrible crash, and, turning around, he saw the lights of the sleeping cars as they fell and disappeared into the darkness below. He ran back to the bridge—and was thunderstruck to find that it was gone. Later that fatal night, he would notice that there was an engraved reproduction of Rembrandt's *Court of Death* on the wall of the train depot telegraph office.

The experience of the passengers and crew, of course, was far more dramatic and painful. Miss Marian Shepard, a survivor, re-

Ashtabula Bridge design sketch.

membered her first hint that something was wrong in her sleeper—the bell rope snapped in two, one piece smashing a whale-oil lamp and the other knocking over a burning candle. A split second later, she heard a bumping noise, as if the train had jumped the tracks and was riding on the wooden ties. Then there was a smashing noise, as if every piece of glass on the train had been shattered to smithereens at once. As all the lights went out, a voice cried, "We are going down!"—and there was a sickening falling sensation. As Miss Shepard braced herself, the air was suddenly filled with flying splinters and dust, as fixtures, seats, lamps, and human bodies were flung about the car, now falling fast, perpendicular to the ground. Seconds later—Marian recalled that it seemed like "two minutes"—her sleeper hit the rest of the No. 5 cars, already wrecked in the frozen waters of Ashtabula Creek.

Marian's experience in the smashed car was a typical one for the terrorized passengers still left alive in the ruined train. Surrounded by the dead who had been killed on impact, she struggled to get out of the dark car, stunned by shock and traumatized by the screams of the wounded. "Every one alive was scrambling and struggling to get out," she recalled. "I heard someone say, 'Hurry out; the car will be on fire in a minute.' Another man shouted, 'The water is coming in, and we will be drowned!'"

It was only too true. Most of the passenger and sleeping cars had fallen like upended dominos, stacked and smashed atop each other, with the bottom layer impaled on the broken ice of Ashtabula Creek. Within five minutes of the crash, the last car, its Baker heater broken but still burning, caught on fire. Dazed, bleeding people staggered out of the pulverized cars, and the winter night was illuminated by flames as, one by one, the No. 5 cars began to burn. Within 15 or 20 minutes, what remained of all 11 cars was a scorching inferno, triggered by the Baker heaters and fed by the train's oil lamps and thickly varnished woodwork.

Many of the survivors were unable to ever forget the terrible scenes they saw that night. As the survivors and rescuers from Ashtabula labored frantically to extricate the wounded and dead from the wrecked train, the flames inexorably moved through the cars, setting one person after another on fire as, foot by foot, their would-be rescuers were driven back. Ironically, at the same time, some of the wounded or trapped passengers were drowning, as the melting waters of the creek crept upward through the mass of bloody, burning debris. Some, perhaps mercifully, would drown before their bodies were thoroughly cremated. Daniel McGuire, who had stopped the "Socrates" 150 feet beyond the bridge and returned to render aid, remembered an especially pitiful sight. A woman trapped by debris screamed over and over as the flames moved toward her, "Take an ax and cut off my legs! Take an ax and cut off my legs!" No one got a chance to perform this awful service for her before she went up in flames and was burned to a crisp. A similar fate awaited a little girl who screamed, "Help me, Mother!" repeatedly as the flames claimed her. Her mother, who already had been pulled from a burning car, could do nothing but watch her child incinerated. Another child was luckier: passed overhead from man to man through a wrecked car, she was eventually handed out of a window to safety. In another case, six men, several of them badly wounded, labored heroically and successfully to free an extremely obese woman who was trapped in a sleeper. They could do little for Peter Levenbroe, the fireman of the "Columbia"; trapped and crushed under a quarter-ton of iron when his engine fell end down and flipped over on its back, he died on the way to a hospital in Cleveland.

The passengers of the "Pacific Express" were not alone in their torment for long.

William Asell, the telegraph operator who had seen the cars fall, immediately made his way to the wreck, half-running, half-falling down the steep, snow-covered hill to the burning railroad pyre. Kicking out windows, he began to pull wounded and often unconscious passengers out, desperately dragging them from the path of the flames. Meanwhile, engineer Daniel McGuire, having brought the "Socrates" to a screeching halt west of the bridge, sprinted the remaining 900 feet to the crowded depot with the terrible news: "Great God, the train is over the bridge, all but us!" A minute later, brakeman A. L. Stone, who had escaped from the last car, limped into the depot. He was hurt and bleeding but frantic that a telegram be sent to Erie in case another train was coming behind. Meanwhile, within minutes, every bell in Ashtabula was sounding the alarm for firemen and rescuers to come to the scene.

The progress of the fire, which ultimately killed more people than the initial crash, has been a source of acrid controversy ever since the moment the first tongues of flame sprang up in the rear car. Although the Ashtabula fire department managed to drag at least one engine down the difficult terrain to the fire, no hoses were ever connected to any available hydrants, and no water, except for a few random buckets of melted snow, was ever thrown at the burning wreck. It was rumored then and afterwards that Lake Shore & Michigan Southern officials, some of whom were on the train or at the depot, expressly forbade anyone to put out the fire. The reason, according to the rumor, was that the company's insurance liability would be less if the passengers were not only dead, but burned beyond recognition. There was no truth to the rumor, but it added a special nastiness to the nightmare of recrimination that followed. The less dramatic truth lay in the confused conditions at the unprecedented conflagration. When Ashtabula fire chief G. A. Knapp arrived at the scene, at least 45 minutes after the crash, he found a scene of pandemonium. (Knapp's personal perception was possibly affected by what a contemporary chronicler characterized as his addiction "to the constant use of intoxicating liquors.")

There was no organized effort to do anything: Passengers and rescuers were simply trying to save such persons as they could, harried as they were by fire, smoke, water, snow, and the difficult terrain. Efforts to deal with the situation were further impeded by hundreds of spectators who crowded the stone abutments above and thronged the panic-stricken spectacle below. Not to mention the activities of thieves, including some who boldly robbed the wounded and helplessly crippled passengers. The terror of those at ground zero was increased by a terrible snapping noise produced by the paint on the train cars as it ignited. Knapp looked around at the chaos and then asked the L. S. & M. S. station agent George Strong which side of the burning wreck he and his men were supposed to throw water on. On hand were 1,500 feet of hose that could be connected to hydrants from 1,000 to 1,200 feet away. Strong, mindful that the advancing flames were consuming more and more people even as they talked, replied that he "didn't want any water, wanted help to get people out." It was probably the right decision. By the time both fire apparatus and personnel were on the scene, the wreck—most of it compact in one sloppy stack of burning cars—was a fully engaged inferno. Without any effort to throw water, the firemen and bystanders concentrated all efforts on trying to pull the wounded from potential watery or fiery graves. No actual orders by Knapp, Strong, or any Ashtabula city officials were issued at the disaster site throughout that long, agonizing night. The fire eventually burned itself out, by morning leaving only a blackened mass of bent iron, festooned with scraps of burned baggage and human flesh.

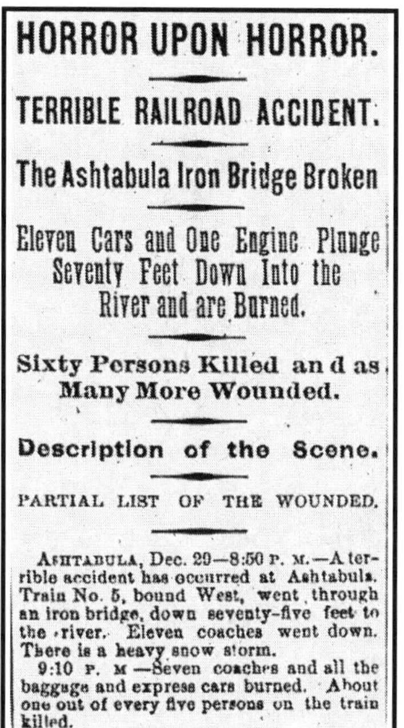

HORROR UPON HORROR.

TERRIBLE RAILROAD ACCIDENT.

The Ashtabula Iron Bridge Broken

Eleven Cars and One Engine Plunge Seventy Feet Down Into the River and are Burned.

Sixty Persons Killed and as Many More Wounded.

Description of the Scene.

PARTIAL LIST OF THE WOUNDED.

ASHTABULA, Dec. 29—8:50 P. M.—A terrible accident has occurred at Ashtabula. Train No. 5, bound West, went through an iron bridge, down seventy-five feet to the river. Eleven coaches went down. There is a heavy snow storm.

9:10 P. M.—Seven coaches and all the baggage and express cars burned. About one out of every five persons on the train killed.

From the *Plain Dealer*, December 30, 1876.

It took almost a week to clean up the mess. Although railway officials quickly had 150 men on the scene to tidy it up and replace the bridge, they never did find or identify the bodies of everyone missing. The chief problem was no one actually knew how many were on the train; the conductor's records showed 128 passengers, but other observers claimed upwards of 200 were aboard when the cars went down. The best guess is that there were 89 killed and 63 wounded, of whom five died later. Nineteen corpses or parts thereof were never identified at all, which is just as well, as the opinion of contemporary spectators was that those found looked like "charred logs" or "Egyptian mummies." A temporary morgue was set up in the Lake Shore & Michigan Southern freight depot, where for several weeks sobbing relatives searched through rows of boxed human remains for their missing loved ones. Many of them could be identified only from earrings, rings, and other items of jewelry that had escaped the attention of thieves attracted to the disaster scene. After funeral services were conducted at two Ashtabula churches on January 19, 1877, the 19 unidentified dead were buried in nearby Chestnut Grove Cemetery. In the 1890s a movement sprang up to memorialize the victims, culminating in the dedication of an impressive 37-foot gray Vermont marble obelisk. Among those who donated to cover the cost were Governor William McKinley and Lucretia Garfield, widow of the murdered president.

The recriminations and investigations began while the fires were still smoldering in Ashtabula Creek. At 9 a.m. the day after the accident, an inquest convened under the authority of justice of the peace Edward W. Richards. Sixty-eight days and dozens of witnesses later, the jury reached a series of eight verdicts, all highly critical of both the Lake Shore railroad and the rescuers at the scene. The controversies generated by their findings still reverberate passionately 130 years later.

The inquest jury found the railway company entirely responsible for the accident, and the consequent deaths and injuries. The jury charged that the L. S. & M. S. had willfully designed, constructed, and erected a fatally flawed bridge and then failed to adequately inspect it over the next 11 years, leading to an inevitable disaster. Additionally, they found that the railway company, in direct violation of an Ohio law of May 4, 1869, had failed to heat its passenger cars "by heating apparatus so constructed that the fire in it will be immediately extinguished whenever the cars are thrown from the track." Lastly, the jury blamed fire department and railway officials at the disaster scene for many of the fire deaths, claiming that they should have concentrated on putting the flames out, rather than rescuing the trapped victims.

None of those accused of malfeasance took it lying down. The Lake Shore and Michigan Southern Railroad eventually paid off about $500,000 in damage claims with little haggling or dispute. But it refused to admit responsibility for the bridge failure, arguing from the first that the wreck was caused either by the "Columbia" leaving the track, a broken rail, or, even more implausibly, a tornado which swooped down to detach the bridge and swooped away again. Most vociferous in rejecting blame was Amasa B. Stone Jr., Cleveland millionaire and railroad mogul—the man who had designed and erected the fatal bridge. Until the day he died, he insisted that it was a sound bridge, flawlessly executed, and that it must have been human error or an act of God that took the "Pacific Express" and his bridge to their ruin.

Stone was wrong, but the truth was a little more complex than either side was willing to allow. The original L. S. & M. S. Ashtabula Creek bridge was a wooden one. In 1863, Amasa Stone made plans to replace it with a new design of his own. The key section was the middle span, a 154-foot section that sat on two stone abutments put up after extensive fill-in narrowed the river valley. It was a variation on the widely used Howe wood-and-iron truss, but Stone's radical redesign made it an all-iron structure, a type that had never been tried and, indeed, would never be replicated. The new structure, installed in the fall of 1865, was a series of 14 panels, protected against the force produced by the weight of the trains by enormous diagonal I-beams, 21 feet in length, which were anchored by three-foot-wide bearing blocks. All of the steel for the bridge was produced at the Cleveland Rolling Mill owned by Amasa Stone's brother Andros. There were many difficulties encountered in installing the bridge, and it had to be completely taken down and put back up again at great expense. When Joseph Tomlinson, an engineer working for Stone, cautioned him about the stress on the trusses, Stone responded by firing him, a move he later blamed on Tomlinson's "inefficiency." The bridge was finished in 1865, tested by the weight of six locomotives, and pronounced perfectly safe. The stage was set for the 1876 tragedy.

As a number of persons later remarked, the strange thing about the fatal bridge was not that it eventually fell, but that it stayed up for 11 years. It was inspected four times a year by L. S. & M. S. officials, who reported no defects, except for an unexplained "snapping" noise train engineers sometimes heard as they sped over the bridge. Among the details missed by the inspectors, no doubt, were the ends of the beams and lugs, where metal had been crudely filed down to make them fit. The bridge was looked at by Charles Collins, the engineer in charge of that stretch of the railroad, just 10 days before the calamity, and he found nothing amiss. What he might have discovered, if he had gotten down among the I-beams, is what Joseph Tomlinson saw when the ruined bridge was lying on the ground 70 feet below two months later: Several of the diagonal I-beams were as much as three inches out of alignment at their juncture with the bearing blocks. Given that the essence of the bridge's design was the interreliance of all its parts, the displacement of the I-beams meant it was just a question of time before something terrible happened.

Charles McDonald subsequently conducted an examination of the tragedy for the American Society of Engineers. His study pinpointed a flaw in one of the large bearing blocks—probably a large, hidden air pocket produced in the casting process—that led to the failure of the supporting beams.

Stone would have none of it, and was his usual adamant, arrogant, and choleric self when interviewed by a special investigative committee of the Ohio legislature on January 18, 1877. Not only was the bridge safe, he insisted to his questioners, it was probably stronger than it needed to be. And as for the Baker stoves that set the cars afire in direct violation of state law, he blustered that he had examined some of the alternative patent stoves available and dismissed them as unsuitable. "My opinion," he stated to his respectful audience of Gilded Age legislators, "is that no stove could be provided which would extinguish its fire in case of accident." "I never shirk responsibility," he concluded, but his final opinion was that the train had simply jumped the track and smashed the bridge to pieces.

There was at least one Lake Shore official with a more tender conscience. Charles Collins, the chief engineer who had recently inspected the failed bridge, "wept like a baby" when he saw the human and material wreckage still smoking in the Ashtabula River

Stereoscopic view of the wrecked train.

valley. Although he testified in public that he had always thought the bridge safe, there were rumors that he had told a different story to his friends. One anecdote had him cynically remarking the year before, "If it goes down, I trust it will be with a freight and not with a passenger train." A more likely public statement was attributed to Collins in the wake of the tragedy, when he felt himself the target for all of the blame hurled by the public at the L. S. & M. S. officials: "Here I have been working 30 years for the protection of the public and now they turn right around and kick me for something which I have had nothing to do with."

Whether Collins actually said these things is debatable, but there is no question he took the bridge disaster uncommonly to heart. Three days after he testified to the special committee, he was found dead in his bed at his residence at Seneca Street (West 3rd) and St. Clair Avenue. Armed with two pistols, he had blown his brains out by firing one of them through the roof of his mouth sometime in the hours just after he finished his testimony. The decomposed state of his body suggested that he had come right home from his ordeal and killed himself.

There were, fortunately, some positive long-term effects from the Ashtabula Bridge disaster. Although there was a brief flurry of agitation for more stringent regulation of railroad safety, nothing ensued immediately except some studies and recommendations authorized by the Ohio legislature. Eventually, however, the beginnings of government oversight, based in part on insights gained from the 1876 accident, were incorporated in the Interstate Commerce Act of 1887. In the meantime, moreover, railway bridge construction had taken a safer, more conservative turn, with most engineers relying on the more reliable Pratt truss. They may not have been impressed by the threat of government interference as much as they were by the half-million dollars in liability paid out by the L. S. & M. S. after the accident.

Destiny finally caught up with irascible Amasa Stone Jr., also. Although he fiercely disclaimed responsibility for the accident and avoided personal legal consequences for it, there is no question that he was hurt by public perception of him as a murderer. His temperament, never a happy one, soured further as ill health and business reverses pressed him harder and harder in the years after the Ashtabula disaster. By 1883, he had endured enough: On the afternoon of May 11 he locked himself in the bathroom of his palatial Euclid Avenue mansion and fired a .32 caliber bullet through his heart.

There is little trace today of the terrible events of December 29, 1876, in the Ashtabula River valley where it happened. The dirty river flows sluggishly under a modern and quite undistinguished viaduct, and it is almost impossible to envision that incredible night of pain, terror, and death. There is a man named Bill Yenne, though, who sees glamour where others might find just a boring landscape. According to his book *Hidden Treasure* (1992), the "Pacific Express" No. 5 train may have been carrying two million dollars in gold bullion that frigid December night. If so, it was all lost in the valley below, waiting still for the right person to find it.

# ASH WEDNESDAY FOREVER

## The Collinwood School Fire

## (1908)

There is no more terrible a story in the annals of Cleveland than the Collinwood school fire. News of the disaster was heard round the world when it happened, and it has lost neither its horror nor its pathos in the nearly 90 years since it first stunned Clevelanders with its unprecedented—and still unsurpassed—toll of death and suffering, the most woeful Cleveland story ever. Still echoing down through the years is the cry of a grey-haired, grief-stricken man who, fourscore years ago, fell to his knees on a Collinwood street and cried, "Oh God, what have we done to deserve this?"

Like many an American metropolis, Cleveland grew throughout the 19th and early 20th centuries by gobbling up smaller, less dynamic villages, hamlets, and neighborhoods. In the early 1900s, many Clevelanders were convinced that the natural eastern limit of their city should be Euclid Creek, and so it was that city authorities increasingly focused on annexing the village of North Collinwood as the century's first years unfolded. Acquisition of Collinwood would bring Cleveland to the borders of Euclid Village, and most Collinwood residents, too, thought such an incorporation would happen sooner or later. A railroad town that grew up around the tracks of the Lake Shore & Michigan Southern Railroad, North

Collinwood grew from a population of 2,500 in 1890 to about 7,500 in 1908. The village was badly strained by the demands of its growing population, and was increasingly hard pressed to provide even basic services like fire protection and education.

Nowhere was the insufficiency of village resources more manifest than at Lakeview Elementary School. Opened in the fall of 1901, the three-story school on Collamer Avenue (now East 152nd Street) had originally served fewer than 200 students in four classrooms. Surging enrollment necessitated construction of an additional four classrooms in 1907, and by the spring of 1908, 350 pupils were housed in those eight classrooms, with a fifth-grade class in the third-floor auditorium.

After the tragedy of the fire, virtually everyone agreed that the construction of the Lakeview Elementary School was unsafe (it certainly was by modern standards), but no one remarked on its dangers at the time. Certainly not the city fathers, who had to pay for the rather impressive-looking structure of wood and brick. Certainly not the architect of the original four-room structure, John Eisenman. Nor did the architects who expanded the building, Searles, Hirsh & Gavin, comment on its structural perils. In fact, Lakeview was probably no better or worse than most schools of the day—as Cleveland officials subsequently found when fears raised by the Collinwood tragedy highlighted similar dangers in Cleveland schools.

Built on a foundation of red brick and framed with Norway pine, the eight-classroom school was oriented on an east-west axis, with its front exit facing Collamer Avenue. Stairways made of Georgia yellow pine led down from the first floor to front and rear exits, identically constructed with two sets of swinging double doors separated by five-foot-deep vestibules. Although the vestibules were ten feet, eight inches wide, they had two-foot-six-inch-wide partitions on each side—so the total width of the attached swinging doors was only a little over five feet. (All of the swinging doors, contrary to subsequent rumor, opened outward, not inward.) The most dangerous component of the front and rear exits was the

Collinwood school fire, March 4, 1908.

area between the bottom of the stairs and the first pair of swinging doors: it was only a couple of feet from the last stair to the inner doors, and anyone exiting had to turn slightly to the right in front of the partition to reach the first set of doors.

The school basement contained a furnace and boiler—located at about the middle of the building, separate washrooms for the boys and girls, and some small rooms for storage. Only the basement, hallways, and vestibules had electric lights; the eight classrooms and two teachers' lounges relied on coal-oil lamps for illumination. The school was maintained and kept clean by janitor Fritz Hirter, a 46-year-old immigrant from Switzerland, who himself had three children enrolled there. Much beloved by the Lakeview children, Hirter was also lauded by their parents for the meticulous care he lavished on the school and its grounds.

March 4, Ash Wednesday, began much like any other school day at Lakeview. It was pleasant weather for late winter, a little windy but sunny and clear, with a high of 36 degrees expected. About 7:30 a.m., Fritz Hirter walked the three blocks from his home on Collamer Avenue to the school and unlocked the outer doors. After stoking the furnace to make sure the building would be warm enough, he went about his usual routine of sweeping the stairs, rooms, and hallways. Sometime after his arrival, Hirter discovered three girls in the school basement playing hide and seek or tag, and shooed them out. Later he would remember only their first names—Mary, Anna, and Lizzie—and no one will ever know what they were actually doing down there.

About 8:00 a.m., the nine Lakeview teachers began to arrive and prepare for the day's lessons. They included Pearl Lynn, who taught a class of 34 first graders in a first-floor room at the southwest corner of the building; Grace Fiske, who taught 40 first graders in the northwest corner across from Lynn; Ethel Rose, who taught 39 second graders in the southeast corner of the first floor, and Ruby Irwin, whose fourth-grade class of 38 occupied the northeast room opposite Rose's. Up on the second floor were Katherine Gollmer's fifth-grade class of 44 in the northwest corner; Katherine Weiler's 39 second graders in the southwest room; Lulu Rowley's class of 35 third graders in the southeast room, and principal Ann Moran's taught 41 sixth graders in the northeast corner room. On the third floor, Laura Bodey taught 41 fifth graders in the former auditorium, now converted to class space because of the overcrowding.

Fire safety was not neglected at Lakeview. There had been at least three fire drills since September, although Laura Bodey later testified that there had not been one since she had arrived at Lakeview in mid-February, and evidence suggests that there had not been a fire drill since Christmas, because of inclement weather. In the event of a fire, janitor Hirter was supposed to ring a bell in Ruby Irwin's northeast first-floor room that set off bells on the second and third floors. The fire signal was three rings; after that, Hirter was supposed to make sure the sets of double doors at both exits were wide open. At the sound of the fire bell, the children were to arise from their seats, assemble in a double column at the side of each room, and proceed to either the front or rear exits in an assigned pattern. As was the usual custom in schools, the younger grades were concentrated closer to the exits, with all the first graders on the first floor. The classes exiting from the second and third floors were trained to wait on the stairs until the first-floor classes had exited the building. There was also a fire escape on the north side of the building, accessible from some of the second-floor classroom windows. The experience of past fire drills suggested that the building could be emptied in about 90 seconds.

The school day officially began at 8:45 a.m. Janitor Hirter later recalled checking the boiler pressure and adding some coal to keep the heat up just before 9:30; he remembered nothing amiss as the school settled into the day's routine. But at about 9:40, while Hirter was sweeping the basement, Emma Neibert, 13, came down the front basement stairs from the third floor to use the girls' washroom. She had only gotten down a few steps when she noticed a puff of smoke. (Hirter would later describe it as no more smoke than one would see at the end of a cigar.) She halted on the second step and called out to Hirter, whom she could see dimly in the basement, "What's the matter?" She received no reply and called again. A split second later, she saw him run by her and race up the front stairs. Seconds later, he rang the fire bell in Ruby Irwin's classroom, which was the closest to the front stairs, and then ran out to open both sets of front and rear doors. And so the Collinwood school fire tragedy began.

The evacuation began well. Ethel Rose's second graders arose from their desks, formed a double line, and followed their teacher safely out into the hall and down the front stairs, physically blocking the stairs to the basement, where flames were already licking hungrily at the tinder-dry pine risers. All of Rose's pupils escaped safely, and her later memory was that both sets of doors at the front exit were wide open. Almost as soon as Rose's class was out, though, flames began to seal off the front-door exit.

Right behind Rose's second graders came Ruby Irwin's 38 first graders. By this time the stairs down to the front exit were in flames. Irwin ordered her pupils to run through the flames to safety. Some of them did, and they survived the day. But most panicked, wheeled around, and began to run toward the rear-door exit. Within seconds, Irwin was driven back from the stairs by the mounting flames and watched helplessly as most of her pupils dashed for the rear exit. She managed to corral some of them and led them into one of the first-floor classrooms. Opening a window, she lowered the children to the ground, one by one, before leaping to safety herself. Some of her pupils who ran to the rear exit also escaped out of other windows on the first floor.

The fatal nexus of the Collinwood fire developed at the rear (west) exit shortly after the attempted evacuation of Ruby Irwin's class. Some of Irwin's pupils ran into children exiting from both the rear first-floor rooms and the four second-floor classrooms. Someone stumbled at the bottom of the stairs by the rear exit, and within seconds screaming, writhing children began to pile up right in front of the first set of rear school doors. Those doors, like the outer pair, were probably both open at the time—but the space was so tight at the turn by the stairs that no one could get through the mounting barrier of human flesh.

Laura Bodey guided her third-floor class of 41 fifth graders down the front stairway. By the time they reached the second floor, it was already filled with smoke. Bodey turned the class around—except for a few who panicked and fled down the stairs to join the fatal congestion at the front exit—and led them into a second-floor classroom. There was a fire escape adjacent to one of the windows there, and Bodey began to evacuate the children, repeating over and over, "The fire escape. Girls first." One by one, Bodey lowered the children from the end of the fire escape, six feet above the ground. Only six of her children died that day, all of them ones who had run to the front exit.

By now, only minutes into the fire, both the front and rear exits had become impassable. Second-floor classes coming down the stairs had collided with panicked children on the first floor, and both exits were blocked with bodies of dead and dying children in the areas between the stairs and the inner sets of doors. Some children survived by hurling themselves from the banisters over the

Diagram of rear door and partition of Lakeview School. *Cleveland Press,* March 6, 1908.

rising pile of writhing bodies. But most of them soon joined the fatal masses by the doors, many of those at the bottom suffocating long before the flames reached them.

First-grade teacher Pearl Lynn got her 34 pupils out into the hall in good order. But as they reached the back stairs, some of them panicked, and she was knocked down the stairs toward the first set of doors. Children began to pile up on top of her. She later recalled her descent toward death: "All in an instant I was borne down, caught and held as in a vise. The incredible thing was the awful swiftness of the horror. How I got out I don't know. I must have been pulled loose somehow. By that time every stick of woodwork on the first floor was burning."

It's understandable that Lynn could not recall her escape: by the time she was pulled out her clothes were torn to pieces and she was in a state of near-suffocation. She was rescued by Fritz Hirter and Lake Shore Railroad shopman Frank Dorn, one of the first rescuers to arrive at the school. Risking his life, Dorn pulled Lynn and 17 others out of the blocked front and rear exits. Lynn's arms were badly burned but she survived the fire.

Katherine Weiler's second-floor class of second graders was doing its arithmetic lesson when the fire bell rang. Weiler managed to lead them to the stairs, but they panicked when they got there and began surging down toward the seething mass of children at the back door. Weiler waded into the screaming mob, saying "Quiet, children. Quiet. Go back to the fire escape." She was still trying to get them to turn around and go into one of the first-floor rooms when she was knocked down the back stairs by the crush of children still pouring down the stairs from the second floor. Her body was never found.

Grace Fiske's first-floor class of first graders was normally routed to the front exit, but when she got them there it was already impassable. She turned them around and led them to the back exit, only to find it blocked from floor to ceiling with dead and dying children. Fiske tried to get children to go into a classroom with her and then waded into the blockage, trying to pull children free. Like Weiler, she was eventually knocked down near the rear exit doors and burned to death with the children she tried to save. When last seen, she was attempting to shelter two terrified children from the advancing flames within the folds of her voluminous skirt.

Lulu Rowley later remembered that when the fire bell rang, she stood up, said, "Partners, quick! Don't rush!" and had one of her third graders open the classroom door. Thick smoke immediately poured into the room, and some of the children broke from their lines and ran down the front staircase. The staircase was already blocked, so Rowley tried to lead the remnants of her class into a first-floor room and out a window. The few that went with her got out to safety. Rowley then tried to get to the back exit to save more children, but it was hopelessly blocked. She eventually escaped out a back window on the first floor. One of Rowley's pupils, Harold Echelberger, remembered the scene after the fire bell rang this way:

> The boys in my room cried out "False alarm, false alarm." Miss Rowley told them to sit still and be quiet. At this time the room was filled with smoke and all the children were screaming and yelling, and finally they broke away from the control of the teacher and rushed out into the hall and down the stairway . . . Herbert Grant and I dove head first down the stairway over the mass of children who were lying underneath us. I don't know how I got out. Somebody seemed to grab us and pull us outside. I saw little children putting out the fire on their hair with their hands. They were screaming for their parents and teacher while the flames were creeping all around them.

Katherine Gollmer got her class of 44 fifth graders out of their rear second-floor classroom. But she lost control of them as they reached the staircase, most of them charging down the stairs to die at the blocked rear exit. Gollmer managed to persuade some of them to go with her into a second-floor classroom. There she found principal Ann Moran, who had just endured a similar experience with her sixth-grade class of 41. Moran could not stop them from fleeing to the fatal staircases, though she eventually managed to drag a few children into a room. Together, she and Gollmer smashed a window with a chair and started lifting children onto the fire escape. Moran later recalled the tragic contrast that emerged as the fire progressed:

> I ran out into the hall and beheld the most pathetic sight my eyes have ever seen. The children were marching past the door in perfect order, heads up and feet keeping time. Their teachers were beside them, keeping the lines straight. The little ones were

> smiling and happy. They thought it was a fire drill. A moment later the vanguard reached the first floor. They saw the flames leaping from the basement. They screamed, broke ranks, and ran for the front door.

The doom of 172 Lakeview children—about half the enrollment of 350 or so—was sealed within scant minutes of the fire's outbreak. The blaze, which probably started in a small storage room beneath the front stairs, may have been smoldering for some time before Emma Neibert first saw smoke at 9:40 a.m. Cleveland fire chief George A. Wallace later opined that the wood in the building, tinder dry from proximity to inadequately shielded and spaced heating pipes, had been "cooking" for weeks before the actual fire. In any case, the structure was fully engaged within 15 minutes, a lost cause within a half hour, and a completely gutted ruin within an hour. Aiding the spread and force of the flames was a brisk northeast wind, which blew like a bellows through the eastern back doors and the many windows opened or broken in frantic escape attempts.

Rescue attempts began almost immediately. They were much hampered by the fact that no one in the neighborhood seemed to have a ladder that could reach the school windows, or an axe to chop away the deadly partitions at the swinging exit doors. John Leffel was probably the first rescuer to arrive. Walking by the school, he saw smoke and began to run. When he got to the rear exit, it was already jammed with bodies at the foot of the stairs. He began pulling children out of the screaming mass and was soon joined by janitor Hirter and several other men. Leffel recalled:

> Some of the children seemed to be half-suffocated. Some were unconscious. I did not stop to look. I seized them by the arms or legs and tossed them out behind. I guess there were others to pick them up and carry them out of the way. The flames were rushing upon us and I knew we had only a few moments left. Many of the children were still piled up in the entrance when

The Cleveland Press. EXTRA

# 125 CHILDREN PERISH IN BURNING SCHOOL HOUSE

DEAD

North Collinwood School Destroyed and Little Ones, Caught Like Rats in Trap, Die in the Flames.

*Cleveland Press* headline, March 4, 1908.

the heat and smoke drove us back from them.

One of those trapped children was Edna Hirter, the Lakeview janitor's eight-year-old daughter. As Hirter labored frantically with other rescuers to pull children out of the blocked rear exit area, he suddenly caught a glimpse of Edna, trapped just feet away in an impenetrable mass of children. "Papa, oh, Papa! Save me, save me!" she screamed. But Hirter could not get to her; her feet were hopelessly trapped by the entangled arms and legs, and he watched as she burned to death in front of his eyes.

One of the big heroes of the day was Wallace Upton, a nearby resident and owner of much of the orchard property skirting the school. Upton, badly burned as he tirelessly worked to pry children out from the rear exit, saved 18 children that terrible day. Today, a nearby Collinwood street memorializes his courage.

Within minutes of the alarm, hundreds of hysterical Collinwood parents began to converge on the fire scene, soon joined by thousands of Clevelanders who had nothing better to do than congest the area and hamper rescue efforts with their presence. By the time most parents got there, however, there was little they could do except watch, like Fritz Hirter, as their children died right in front of them. One of the unfortunate parents was Mrs. Clara Sprung, who saw smoke at about 9:30 a.m. from her Collamer Avenue home just across the street. Arriving at the school, she saw her son Alvin at a first-floor window, trapped by the advancing flames. Returning with a ladder from her house, she managed to climb to the window and grab Alvin by the hair to pull him out the window. Her efforts were in vain: the fire burned off Alvin's hair in her hands, and he died minutes later in the flames.

There were dozens of similar scenes as anguished parents watched their trapped children die just inches from safety at the front and rear exits. One of them was Mrs. John Phillis, who could not reach her daughter Jennie, 15, caught at the rear exit. "Oh Jennie! Please come out!" screamed Mrs. Phillis. "I can't move, Ma. Oh, help me, if you can!" replied Jennie. Mrs. Phillis watched in heartbreak as the flames crept closer and closer to her daughter. As the flames began to burn Jennie's hair, Mrs. Phillis reached in and began to caress it. Trying to keep the flames away from Jennie's head, she stayed and comforted her dying child until a falling piece of debris almost cut her hand off.

Another parent who tried desperately to save his own child was W. C. Schaeffer. He got to the rear exit and discovered his eight-year-old son, George, trapped in a pile of children. He grabbed George's hands and pulled as hard as he could—but he could not free him from the deadly mass squeezed together at the back doors. Meanwhile, the flames crept closer and closer, and soon George's hair began to catch on fire. His father smothered the flames but they soon rekindled George's hair. Schaeffer would always remember the look in his son's eyes as he sank for the last time in the mass of burning flesh at the rear exit doors.

William Davis of Westropp Avenue was another one of the early rescuers at the rear exit of the school. There he saw a forlorn little girl, wedged into a corner by one of the inner doors. "Mister, help me out," she pleaded. Dodging through the smoke and heat, Davis managed to get close enough to grab her hand and hear her say, over and over, "Mister, save me!" A moment later Davis was knocked down by a piece of falling debris, and the little girl was consumed by the flames only seconds later. As with so many of the girls killed that day, her long hair and long dress aided the rapid spread of the fire around her.

Given the speed with which the flames spread, even quick escape from the school was not enough to save some little lives. Ten-year-old Mildred Schmitt jumped out of a school window, her long skirt in flames up to her knees, screaming, "Papa! Papa!" Bystanders smothered the flames quickly but it was too late: Mildred died a few hours later at Glenville Hospital. Other casualties of the flames lingered longer, but the last survivor, Glen Barber, 8, succumbed to his injuries on Saturday, March 7. He had been caught at the rear door and eventually had jumped from the second floor, injuring himself terribly. His last words before he died were "I am standing on a large rock, larger than all the world."

Some of the greatest heroes of that terrible day were the smallest. Oscar Pahner, 11 years old, escaped out the back exit and, although burned, ran to the Collinwood fire station to report the blaze. He then returned to the school to try to save his sister Edna—in vain. Henry Ellis of Westropp Avenue witnessed another act of sublime heroism when he got to the rear exit, as Ellis recounted to a *Plain Dealer* reporter:

> The fire was creeping up on the children in the rear. I saw one girl, who could not have been more than ten or twelve, protect her little brother, who was not more than six years of age. He cried for help and clung to her hand. She comforted him and covered his head with a shawl she was wearing. The flames were growing closer, and the moans of the children mingled with the crackling of the fire. The little girl drew her brother nearer to her. She saw that there was no help. Together they knelt down on the floor. That was the last I saw. The fire caught them after that.

Another little tragic hero was Frederick Paul. He got out of the school safely but returned to try to save his sister Ruth. Firemen later found them dead together in each other's arms. James Turner, 14, escaped from the first floor by breaking a window and then returned to the inferno to find—and die with—his two little brothers, Norman, 9, and Maxwell, 6. Edna Hebler, 14, also got out alive, only to climb back up the fire escape to find her sister Melba. Edna died in the fire, not knowing that Melba had already arrived home. Janitor Fritz Hirter's 10-year-old son Walter was one of the first children out the school door, but he returned to save his sister Ida, and instead died with her. There were several other documented instances of children who escaped and later perished in the flames when they returned to save siblings or friends.

Collinwood firefighters arrived about 20 minutes into the fire. By now all three floors and the Lakeview basement were in flames, and it is unlikely that any fire department in the world could have saved the remaining children. Some could be seen at the windows of the second and third floors, helplessly trapped and screaming as the flames closed in on them. Some began to jump from the windows. Some survived the fall to the ground, especially those who were caught as they fell by rescuers like A. Hansrath, a local merchant who caught three jumpers. The *Cleveland News* reported that Joseph Neill, a nearby resident, rushed to the school in time to catch 20 children as they jumped from the flames, including his own son, George. More typical, though, was the fate of Mary Ridgeway, Anna Rolth, and Gertrude Davis, who jumped from the third floor and died on impact as they hit the ground. And perhaps the most terrifying sight of the day was the death of Glen Sanderson, a 12-year-old boy trapped on the third floor. A fascinated crowd of hundreds below watched as Sanderson, fleeing from the flames that pursued him across the third floor, swung hand over hand across the third-floor auditorium stage, using pieces of scenery to swing himself toward the fire escape and safety. He got about halfway across the stage, missed his grip, and fell into the flames below.

As the *Plain Dealer* subsequently remarked, the arrival of the

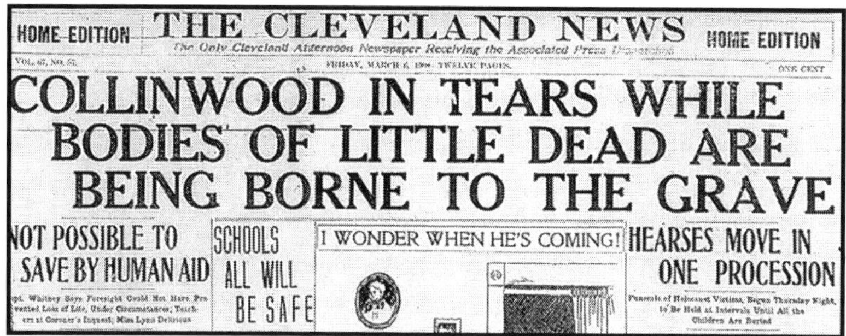

HOME EDITION THE CLEVELAND NEWS HOME EDITION

The Only Cleveland Afternoon Newspaper Receiving the Associated Press

FRIDAY, MARCH 6, 1908. TWELVE PAGES. ONE CENT

COLLINWOOD IN TEARS WHILE BODIES OF LITTLE DEAD ARE BEING BORNE TO THE GRAVE

NOT POSSIBLE TO SAVE BY HUMAN AID

SCHOOLS ALL WILL BE SAFE

I WONDER WHEN HE'S COMING!

HEARSES MOVE IN ONE PROCESSION

Funerals of Holocaust Victims, Begun Thursday Night, to Be Held at Intervals Until All the Children Are Buried

*Cleveland News* headline, March 6, 1908.

Collinwood Fire Department might have been a comic sight under different circumstances. A volunteer force of no more than 10 men, the fire department was an almost pitiable collection of ancient equipment and inefficient vehicles. Moreover, it was delayed because its regular horses were down in South Collinwood pulling a grader, and two horses had to be borrowed from a nearby merchant. And when the firefighters got to the scene—with one hose truck, one engine, and one ladder truck—it was found that their 20-foot ladders couldn't reach the third floor, where many of the children had fled as a last refuge from the flames. Worse yet, there was little pressure in the leaky water lines—no more than 50 pounds per square inch delivered from the nearest fireplug, 150 feet away—and the fire-hose streams could not even reach the second-floor windows. The firemen did the best they could, rescuing those children they could find and reach, but in general their arrival proved the final ghastly irony of a terrible day.

There were hardheaded political reasons, of course, for the pathetic state of Collinwood's fire department. For years an intense struggle had been waged between those who wanted Collinwood annexed by Cleveland and those who did not. Shortly before the fire, the pro-annexation forces had won a victory for their slate, including Mayor Westropp, but the anti-annexationists had managed to delay the actual incorporation indefinitely through a "poison-pill" commission. (Annexation would not become a fact until

January 1910.) In the interim before annexation, neither side was willing to spend any more money on Collinwood's safety forces, as it was assumed that Cleveland would soon take over the duties of fire protection. Cleveland fire units, sent by Chief George Wallace, eventually arrived at the Lakeview fire scene, but too late to do any good.

The climax of the catastrophe came shortly after 10:30 a.m. As hundreds of spectators watched, many with cameras and even, it was said, a moving-picture camera, the first floor collapsed into the basement, followed soon by the second and third floors, burying what was left of more than a hundred children in the smoking rubble of Lakeview Elementary School.

The fire was officially put out by about 1:30 p.m., but firemen and volunteers, many released from the Lake Shore rail yards as soon as word of the fire came, began clearing out the dead and injured as soon as they could safely get into the smoldering wreckage.

One by one the corpses were loaded onto wooden carts, and ambulances from undertakers including Mapes and Shepard helped carry them just south of the school to the Lake Shore Railway Storehouse near Collamer Avenue, which had been turned into a temporary morgue. There, over the next few days, groups of parents—no more than 10 at a time—were brought in to identify the bodies. Corpses of at least 165 children and three adults were taken out of the Lakeview ruins. Some were easily recognizable, others were badly marred by the fire, and still others were little more than pieces of flesh, bone, and clothing that had been raked out of the ruins of the school. Some, like George Schaeffer, were identified by a ring or an earring that the parents remembered and recognized. Others, like Hulda Swanson, 11, were identified by the fillings in their teeth. One child was identified after her parents had spent hours searching in vain; her little dog was admitted to the morgue and immediately ran to the side of his dead, beloved little mistress. It was a horrible business, made more horrible when two sets of parents quarreled over one of the corpses, each insisting that it was their own boy.

Despite vigorous search efforts, the body of Katherine Weiler was never found; presumably it burned to ash in the heat of the rear-exit holocaust, although Barney Reiche of Forster Avenue claimed recalled putting Weiler's body on a stretcher. Also puzzling was the corpse of a young man, at first thought to be Weiler's body and then that of an older boy, until the coroner realized that the teeth were too large. It is likely that it was the body of a man named John Kranjnak of 53 Hale Street. Witnesses saw him run into the burning school to rescue children—and he was never seen alive afterwards.

As preparations for the funerals got under way, the inevitable recriminations began. Many of the bereaved Collinwood parents needed a scapegoat for their tragedy, and they soon focused on janitor Hirter and the surviving schoolteachers. Some of the parents thought it rather suspicious that so few of the teachers had died in the fire, while 172 children, most of them from the second-floor classrooms, had perished. The feeling against Hirter soon grew dangerous, necessitating a guard around his house. Despite the fact that he had lost three of his own children in the fire, it was soon whispered around the village that Hirter had been absent from the school when the fire broke out. Indeed, by the time Coroner Burke got the official inquest under way two days later, Mrs. Julius Dietrich was willing to testify that she had seen Hirter sweeping the porch of his house when she first saw smoke coming from the school and that she next saw him running toward it. There were also repeated allegations by fire witnesses, including several of the Lakeview teachers, that the doors of the school had not been open during the attempted evacuation. These accusations of negligence put Hirter through a terrible ordeal on Burke's witness stand and an even worse one in the court of public opinion. Driven almost to insanity by the loss of his three children and the terrible accusations of his neighbors, the badly burned Hirter could only say, again and again: "Gentlemen, I do not know how the fire started. If you were to kill me, I could not tell you. I do not know. I do not know. I do not know."

For the record, there was never any credible evidence that Hirter was derelict in his duty before, during, or after the fire. Although some witnesses said the school doors were closed during the fire, crucial witnesses testified that they were all open at the onset of the fire, suggesting that the strong wind probably blew them partially or completely shut as the fire progressed. After listening to all of the testimony, Coroner Burke went out of his way to exonerate the beleaguered janitor, issuing a statement on Monday, March 9: "I want to take this occasion to say publicly that the people of Collinwood have no reason to blame you . . . You did not only your duty but you did more than your duty."

Hirter's persecution did not end that day, however. A group of sorrowing mothers, organizing themselves as the "Mothers of the Burned District", attempted to have Hirter fired by the Collinwood School Board. They carried on their campaign against him for some months afterward, some even refusing to send their children to Clark School, where he was reassigned. Hirter eventually went to work for the Cleveland school system, living into the 1950s and dying at the age of 96.

The official inquest and the various fire investigations did little good. Everyone seemed to agree, after the fire, that the Lakeview School should have been fireproofed and that the exit areas should not have been curtailed by partitions. Cleveland fire chief George Wallace asserted that the fire started when a wooden beam in the basement was ignited by an adjacent steam pipe, which had already dangerously dried out much of the school's wood construction in the weeks before the fire. That was also the opinion of the state fire marshals, although no one really knows to this day what set off the Lakeview fire. The final inquest verdict held no one responsible for the blaze, as no Ohio or local law had been broken.

The worst canard to come out of the Collinwood fire was the sturdy legend that the exit doors opened inward, the presumed cause of the fatal pileups at the front and rear. This lie was repeated by at least one state fire marshal on the day after the fire and repeated even by principal Ann Moran—despite the testimony of the

Collinwood school fire, March 4, 1908.

original architect, members of the school board, the architects who expanded the school, fire chief George Wallace, and numerous eyewitnesses of the fatal conflagration. The newspapers picked up the fiction and have repeated it more often than not in the decades since the fire. In 1938, a dogged researcher even dug up the original Lakeview foundations and published archaeological proof that the doors had swung outward. In recent years, other researchers have produced actual period photographs of the exit areas to prove the same point. But the legend endures, and if Clevelanders know only one thing about the Collinwood school fire, it is the untruth that "the doors opened inward."

The funerals of the children began on Thursday and continued through the following Monday. The disaster's impact on the small village of Collinwood was visibly devastating. On some streets, such as Arcade, there was hardly a house without a white ribbon attached to its door knocker, indicating a death. Twenty-three families lost two children each in the fire, and eight families lost three children.

Small wonder that some of the parents soon sank into dangerous depressions. Several of the mothers tried to kill themselves in the days afterward. One of the most determined was Mrs. Amelia Robinson of Forest Avenue. The mother of the only black children who attended Lakeview, she lost both her daughters in the fire. Robinson bitterly reproached the surviving teachers, blaming them for her loss, and tried to throw herself out a second-story window. Restrained, she subsequently tried to hang herself with a quilt.

The last funerals were held on Monday, March 9, climaxing in a solemn ceremony in Lake View Cemetery. There, in a mass grave near the Euclid Avenue entrance, 21 caskets were interred, 19 of them containing unidentified dead. The Village of Collinwood purchased the burial site, paid at least $60 apiece toward the cost of all the funerals, and eventually erected a ruggedly handsome stone monument to the fire's dead at the Lake View Cemetery gravesite. It's still there and contains a plaque bearing the names of all the dead.

Malign reverberations from the fire continued for some time afterwards. The Collinwood schools did not reopen until September, and when they did—with police guards to protect Hirter and the surviving Lakeview teachers—some of the grieving parents refused to send their children to the three temporary elementary schools conducted in two former saloons and an ex-church. The Mothers of the Burned District subsequently opposed the erection of a proposed new school, Collinwood Memorial, next to the fire site, and the construction of a memorial garden over the ruins of Lakeview School. Said Elizabeth Powers, one of the unreconciled mothers: "The site of the burned school is both sacred and horrible. The ashes of the children still lie in its ruins, It is a grave. I would not send my remaining child to study and play where part of his brother's body lies." Sacred ground or not, the garden was eventually built. After subsequent years of neglect, it has been nicely restored. Collinwood Memorial School, a fireproof structure of 10 rooms, opened in September of 1910. It has been vacant and unused in recent decades, but may yet be restored and redeveloped.

Some good did come out of the Collinwood school fire. Thanks in particular to sensationalistic newspaper coverage in the wake of the disaster, the Cleveland schools were discovered to be largely unsafe firetraps and were accordingly renovated. The effects of the publicity about Collinwood were not confined to Cleveland: the fire made headlines around the United States and the entire world, arousing and energizing the champions of school-building safety wherever the awful story was told. The most unfavorable comment came from German newspapers, which excoriated Americans for the low value they put on human life—especially the lives of the German-American children who had died in the fire. It was probably a similarly invidious motivation that brought Prince Albert von Wurten, the ambassador from Austria-Hungary, to Cleveland on March 10 to inquire into the welfare of his countrymen living in the Collinwood neighborhood.

Finally, like all significant Cleveland disaster stories, the Collinwood school fire had its quota of touching—if somewhat bizarre—incidents. One of the oddest came after Ruby Irwin finally succeeded in getting most of her children to safety through the flames at the front door. She turned around to see one of her female pupils jumping out a window of her classroom at the northeast corner of the first floor. As Ruby stared uncomprehendingly, the little girl marched up to her, handed her a familiar-looking garment, and said in the most matter-of-fact voice, "I went back for your cloak."

# "JUMP, BOYS, IT'S A CRASH!"

## The Doodlebug Deathtrip

## (1940)

People of the modern age like to look back condescendingly at the medieval "Age of Faith"—but its mundane credulities were as nothing compared to the naive confidence we denizens of the 20th century place in the infrastructure of technological systems that make the realities of contemporary life possible. Every day most of us step into machines—airplanes, trains, and automobiles—and let them take us whither we will, secure in the certainty that they will get us there safely and uneventfully. Most of us don't comprehend how these complex machines and systems work, but our confidence in them and the human beings that run them remains generally secure. After all, 999,999 times out of a million, nothing goes wrong, so why shouldn't we persist in our childlike faith in things we don't understand?

This is a story about that one millionth time, when everything that was supposed to work didn't, and the common sense and good judgment that usually prevent our complex world from dissolving into murderous chaos failed. It failed in 1876, when Amasa Stone's pigheaded arrogance placed a defective railroad bridge over Ashtabula Creek. It failed in 1895, when a trolley conductor took Car No. 42 over the edge of an open swivel-bridge on Cleveland's Central Viaduct. It failed in 1916, when safety officials for the waterworks tunnel project ignored the warning signs of explosive methane gas in intake crib No. 5, 128 feet below Lake Erie. It failed in 1929, when an unthinking Cleveland Clinic employee hung an exposed electric light bulb right next to sheets of flammable nitrocellulose X-ray film in a basement record room. And this is the now-forgotten but still terrible story of how it failed in Cuyahoga Falls on July 31, 1940: the fiery tale of the Doodlebug Inferno.

Why it was called a "Doodlebug" remains an elusive question. "Doodlebug" is the slang name given to several species of insects, including a variety of dung beetle. Perhaps it was the shape: although the general outline of the gas-electric vehicle resembled an old-fashioned trolley car, the appearance of its long, bulging gas-line tanks carried underneath suggested the swollen shape of a bug's larvae. Or maybe it was the hybrid, mongrel nature of the self-powered car, which drove itself over the rails with an engine powered by the gasoline it carried below. By 1940 the word was an accepted term in railroad jargon, and users of the one-car commuter service that ran the 12 miles between Hudson and Akron used the term affectionately to describe the train that took them daily to their jobs and homes, and to other trains linking Northeast Ohio to the rest of the nation. Whatever the reason, it wasn't what anyone would call a fair match when the Doodlebug hit the Pennsylvania Railroad FC-4 freight train at 6 p.m. on the dot that last day of July 1940.

Carrying 46 passengers and crew, plus its several hundred gallons of gasoline fuel, the Doodlebug probably weighed 122,000 pounds when it collided with the FC-4. Or rather, the FC-4 collided with it: with 73 loaded freight cars, the FC-4 outmatched the Doodlebug by several million pounds, not to mention its superior momentum. When they collided almost exactly at the Front Street crossing in Cuyahoga Falls, the bulk and force of the FC-4 told immediately. Cleaving the metal-plate skin of the Doodlebug "like a melon" (as one eyewitness described it), the lead locomotive of the FC-4 "telescoped" its way into the crowded Doodlebug, smashing its way through seats, poles, partitions, windows, and human beings as it ploughed relentlessly forward. Forcing the Doodle-

THE WEATHER FORECAST

CLEVELAND NEWS

THURSDAY, AUGUST 1, 1940

THREE CENTS

STOCKS SPORTS

# BLAME COACH CREW AS 43 DIE IN WRECK AT CUYAHOGA FALLS

Aim Bomb At Builder For City

*Harder On Mound in Sox Finale*

*43 Rode to Death in This!*

Daylight view of wrecked car in which 43 of 46 occupants met death

Officials Find Order Which Directed Pair To Halt on Siding

BULLETIN

Charred bodies of 43 persons lay today in mortuaries in Akron and Cuyahoga Falls, victims of a train crew's apparent disregard of safety orders in Ohio's worst train wreck in 64 years.

From the *Cleveland News*, August 1, 1940

bug backward down the screeching rails, the FC-4, its own brakes screaming, didn't come to a stop until it had pushed the punctured car five hundred feet north of the point of impact. Even as the two trains shuddered to a stop, still locked in their lethal embrace, the gasoline tanks under the Doodlebug exploded and drenched both trains in a hot torrent of burning gasoline. Before the gaze of horrified eyewitnesses, the crushed Doodlebug and its human freight began to burn up in pillars of flame that reached out 25 feet from either side of the double wreck and as high into the air. How had this happened?

It certainly shouldn't have, everyone later agreed. When the Doodlebug left Hudson at 5:49 on its regular run to Akron, its route and orders were clear. Engineer Thomas L. Murtaugh had a copy of them, as did conductor Harry B. Shaffer, and their import should have been unequivocal to these experienced railroad men: "Engine 4454—running extra—Arlington to Hudson—to meet No. 3380, gas-engine 4648 at Switch 1, Silver Lake."

What it meant in normal English was that the Doodlebug

(Engine 4648) had a "meet" order with Engine 4454 (FC-4) at the number 1 switch at Silver Lake, several miles north of Cuyahoga Falls. The section of the Pennsylvania Railroad used by both trains was a one-track line, so it was a matter of routine for the southbound Doodlebug to lay over ("meet") on a rail siding at Silver Lake while any northbound train passed it. The Doodlebug could then proceed south, but only after it called Hudson for permission to proceed onto the next "block" or section of track south of Silver Lake. Block operator O. L. Rickey had personally given the "meet" orders to Murtaugh and Shaffer at Hudson, and the crew of the FC-4 was given identical orders at Arlington sometime after 5 p.m.

To this day nobody knows why it happened. Engineer Murtaugh brought the Doodlebug to the number 1 switch at Silver Lake right on schedule. But then, instead of switching to the siding and calling Rickey to get block permission, he just kept right on going. Murtaugh himself would not remember the accident, so why he kept the Doodlebug going south remains a mystery. Neither conductor Harry B. Shaffer, brakeman A. L. Bailiff, nor baggage man Charles Bilderback, all familiar with the run, said anything, and Shaffer later recalled that he was too busy taking tickets from the passengers and checking them off his list to notice anything unusual. But just before 6 p.m., he happened to glance at his watch and looked up to see . . . the outskirts of Cuyahoga Falls instead of the expected view of the Silver Lake siding. As he told it later from his hospital bed: "I jumped up to go up front and find out from Murtaugh why we had passed the siding. Just as I got to my feet, I looked out and saw the locomotive of the freight train rounding the curve ahead, coming toward us. I knew we were going to hit. We were going 50 to 55 miles an hour. I ran back into the baggage compartment and yelled, 'We're going to hit! Jump!' Then I jumped."

Shaffer wasn't the only one who saw the disaster coming. As the lead locomotive of the FC-4 pulled out of the curve just south of the Front Street crossing, engineer O. M. Lodge and fireman E. N. Reynolds suddenly saw the Doodlebug coming at them. Jamming the brakes, Reynolds watched in shock as his train cleaved the Doodlebug's front and began driving it up the track. Simultaneously, Lodge and Reynolds heard the explosion of the Doodlebug's tanks. Seconds later they were covered with a shower of burning gasoline that spread over the first two dozen cars of the FC-4. Stumbling out of their cab and frantically smothering the burning fuel on their skin, they ran toward the flaming Doodlebug.

Wesley Payne probably had the best view of the wreck. Sitting in his '35 Buick at the Front Street crossing gate, he was watching the Doodlebug go by. He didn't see the freight train until it hit the Doodlebug, and he watched in stupefaction as they collided with a terrific crash, burst into showering flames, and started moving northward on the track. Within seconds, Payne's car was covered with burning gasoline. Jumping out, he began running for the nearby Cuyahoga River along with other bystanders, some of whom were on fire. Stumbling down a ravine, Payne injured his left knee and was later stitched up at St. Thomas Hospital. His verdict on the wreck echoed that of everyone else who saw it: "I served in the World War and fought in active battles in France but the confusion and turmoil that followed the explosion was more horrible and ghastly than anything I saw in the war."

What Payne remembered about the horrific scene agreed with the accounts of all who saw the aftermath of the crash. The initial impact of the locomotive and the freight had smashed virtually everything inside the Doodlebug, mixing broken seats, windows, and other debris in a veritable salad of metal ruin. At the same time, it had thrown almost all of the passengers forward toward what was left of the front of the car. (Actually, the "front" was the back, as the dual-control setup of the Doodlebug allowed it to run forward or backward without turning around; it had been traveling "backward" when it hit the FC-4.) They were probably all dead when the first rescuers arrived. Those who came to help remembered that the most macabre aspect of the horrible scene was its unearthly, eerie quiet—there was not a cry, moan, or scream to be heard, only the sound of flames licking hungrily at the Doodlebug wreckage. Witnesses could see the passengers inside, many of them either crammed up against the windows or sticking out through the windows like ripped-open sacks of laundry. And it was just as well they all seemed to be dead because it took some time to get the 43 bodies out. The weight of the collision had warped and bent the sides of the Doodlebug so forcefully that it took crews working with acetylene torches many hours before they could extricate all of the bodies. Not that there was much left of them: although some corpses were thrown clear of the train, many were charred and burned beyond recognition. Jewelry, dental work, and pieces of clothing would eventually identify all the victims.

Miraculously, there were three survivors of the wreck. One was engineer Murtaugh, who apparently saw the FC-4 coming and dived out of the driver's cab before the crash. He fractured his skull and sustained other, minor injuries but survived, unable to understand or recall why he had driven the Doodlebug to its deadly end. Delirious, he was taken to the hospital, where he repeatedly moaned, "Get me out of here, I've got to get back to work." Another who escaped the inferno was conductor Harry Shaffer, who ran back through the baggage compartment, shouting "Jump, boys, it's a crash!" At least that's what Tod E. Wonn, age 24, remembered him saying, even as he watched Shaffer hurtle out the side door. Wonn, a Pennsylvania Railroad section hand, was riding as a "deadhead" passenger, that is, free of charge. Sitting in the baggage area, Wonn didn't even have time to wake his friend, Bruce Kelly, who was sleeping beside him. The trains had already collided when he jumped, and his clothes were on fire when he hit the ground. Rolling through the brush, Wonn managed to extinguish the flames. Stumbling, covered with blood and in shock, Wonn wandered into a filling station run by Fred Eckman near the Front Street crossing. Crying "My buddy, oh my buddy!" Wonn refused to let Eckman's wife, Molly, attend to his wounds, and he ran out of the station and back to the railroad tracks, searching vainly for his dead roommate, Bruce. But Wonn came out of the wreck in better shape than conductor Shaffer, who lost his right hand and foot, probably when the Doodlebug was pushed over them by the FC-4 freight.

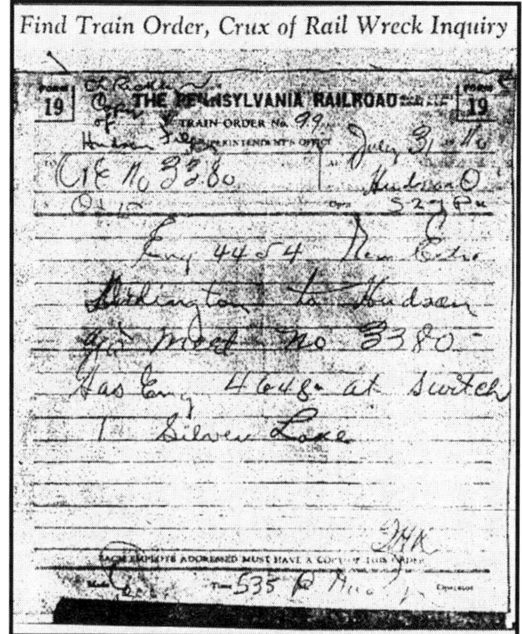

*Find Train Order, Crux of Rail Wreck Inquiry*

19 THE PENNSYLVANIA RAILROAD 19

TRAIN ORDER No. 99

July 31 1940

C & E No 3380

Hudson O

5 27 P M

Eng 4454 Run Extra

Hudson

meet No 3380

Has Eng 4648 at Switch

Silver Lake

Copy of order for the missed layover at Silver Lake.

Local safety forces and many civilians performed well in the emergency. Within minutes, area policemen and sheriff's deputies were drawn to the scene by the sound of the crash and early reports on local radio stations. One of them was L. P. Seller, Cuyahoga Falls fire chief: "I was there two minutes after the wreck and the Doodlebug was already a furnace. I heard no screams and realized everyone inside was dead. Some victims were hanging partly out of the windows and they were on fire. Some were pushed out by the force of the freight still pushing and they littered the tracks on either side. They were all shattered, bleeding, and burnt. The interior looked as though a tornado hit it."

Especially heroic and grisly was the work of the men who brought the bodies out. Working for hours to cut them out of the twisted metal, they endured sights and sensations rarely seen outside a devastated battlefield. And their work wasn't made any easier by the behavior of the many ghouls who soon showed up to gawk at the wreckage. Before the day was finished, as many as 20,000 people would converge on the scene, significantly hampering the work of safety forces, who repeatedly had to drive the crowds back with force. Perhaps the person who best kept her cool and rendered useful service that day was Molly Eckman, who tried to help the dazed Tod Wonn when he stumbled into her husband's station. Living only 80 feet from the point of impact, Molly had been washing dishes when she heard the familiar tootle of the Doodlebug and looked up to see the passengers at the windows looking back at her. Seconds later, she heard the crash, and the next thing she saw was the Doodlebug going by in the opposite direction. As soon as she saw it burst into flames, Molly ran to her linen closet and got all the towels she could carry. "I knew they would need bandages," she later explained. Heading toward the tracks, she could feel the heat as thc burning gasoline did its pitiless work. Another who acted well was the Reverend Joseph Butler, an assistant priest at St. John's Cathedral in Cleveland. Visiting friends in Cuyahoga Falls, he heard sirens and went to the scene of the crash. Standing by the ruined car and performing his creed's rite for any Catholic dead who might have been on board, he offered conditional absolution as each of the bodies was brought out of the wreckage.

It only took firemen about 15 minutes to get the flames out when they finally arrived on the scene about 20 minutes after the crash. There were some anxious moments, particularly for the FC-4 crew, as they watched the burning gasoline moving toward the fully loaded petroleum tank cars of the 73-car train. But engineer Lodge and fireman Reynolds, ignoring their own burns, stayed on the scene and helped direct the efforts of firemen to contain the danger to the freight train. Oddly, considering the fate of the Doodlebug, the collateral damage from the accident was minor. Although the railroad ties were partially burned for a length of 500 feet, the rails themselves held firm, and the single-track line was returned to normal service by the following morning.

Summit County coroner R. E. Amos and his aides dealt with the

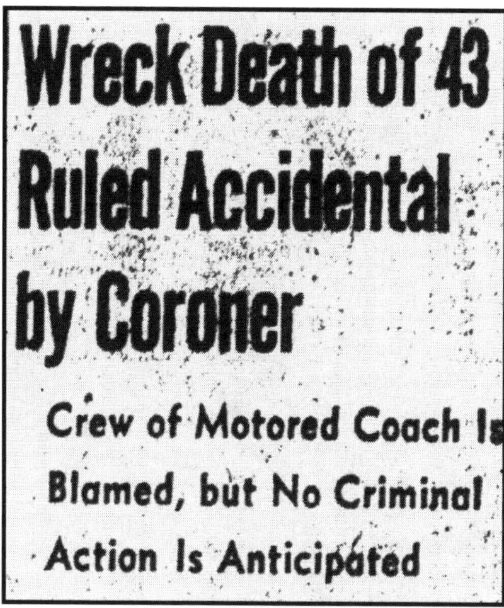

Wreck Death of 43 Ruled Accidental by Coroner

Crew of Motored Coach Is Blamed, but No Criminal Action Is Anticipated

From the *Cleveland Press*, August 2, 1940

aftermath of the tragedy in methodical, professional fashion. Supervising the long hours of bringing out the dead, Amos had workers stack pocketbooks, glasses, briefcases, and burned clothing carefully, so as to aid in identification of the bodies. Moving briskly, Amos got the inquest under way the next morning. As engineer Murtaugh and conductor Shaffer were too badly injured to testify, the evidence available to the panel was limited and secondary. But Amos managed to file a report the very next day, finding that the crash had occurred because Murtaugh and Shaffer had disobeyed their written orders. It would appear that Amos, for lack of any better testimony, relied on the views of F. W. Krick, Pennsylvania Railroad division superintendent, who stated: "Apparently, both the engine man and conductor on [the Doodlebug] had proper orders to wait at the Silver Lake siding and let the freight train pass. But apparently both of them had a mental lapse at the same time."

After conferring with Summit County prosecutor Alva R. Russell, Amos ruled that Murtaugh and Shaffer could not be prosecuted, as the wreck involved "no specific violation of any statute." The entire matter was just a case of mass "accidental death." Additional probes by Pennsylvania Railroad officials, the Ohio Public Utilities Commission, and the Interstate Commerce Commission added nothing significant to the solution of the Doodlebug puzzle.

Conductor Shaffer blamed the whole thing on Murtaugh's oversight, and Murtaugh himself couldn't remember a thing. But Murtaugh's wife defended him stoutly to newspaper reporters, saying: "I am certain that when he took the Doodle-Bug on that main line he was doing it under orders. I know him well enough to be sure that if he had had orders to stop at a siding he would have stopped. I am certain that if he was able to defend himself from these charges he would say that he had no such orders . . ."

Unfortunately for Murtaugh, Shaffer's duplicate copy of his orders was found in the wreck, confirming the theory that he had, for unknown reasons, ignored his orders. But both Murtaugh and Shaffer had other defenders during the firestorm of recrimination that ensued from the Doodlebug wreck. Speaking for the Brotherhood of Railway Trainmen on August 5, legislative representative George A. Fox blamed the accident on the Pennsylvania Railroad's cost-cutting practices. Stating that there had previously been three signalman stationed on the 12-mile Hudson-Akron line, Fox declared that the accident would not have happened if the Pennsylvania Railroad had not eliminated the signalmen jobs as an economizing measure: "We can't agree that this crew with long experience on the line could have made a mistake in such explicit procedure. We have been in constant dispute with the railroad to assign operators to the signal stations. We've maintained that it's not the business of an engineer or a conductor to do the work of an operator. . . . Whenever a safety measure is required costing money, the railroads invariably resist installing it and they come around to it only because the trainmen's organizations put pressure on them."

And that was that. The mess was cleaned up, the dead were eulogized and buried, and Doodlebug service was soon restored to the Akron-Hudson line. Ironically, the train made its last run on

July 31, 1951, exactly 11 years to the day after the Cuyahoga Falls catastrophe. Today, virtually no one remembers either the Doodlebug or the fiery tragedy that took 43 lives. So let the last words go to Dr. Charles D. De Gruchy, an eyewitness, who uttered the most eloquent account of the horror:

> I was on my way home to Silver Lake when the crossing lights caused me to stop my car. The Doodle came sailing along and I thought nothing about it until I happened to turn my head and saw the freight bearing down from the other direction. . . . The flasher light was going—there was no screeching of brakes [Author's note: most witnesses heard the brakes screech]—there was no warning signal from either train. The locomotive just seemed to disappear into the Doodler . . . there was a crash—a terrific explosion and a shower of splotches of flames like maple leaves falling in the autumn breeze. Glass fell like hail—or like someone threw a bucketful of buckshot. . . . I went back to the train where a few people had gathered. I saw the bodies packed around the nose of that locomotive right to the roof. The steam and flames shot out all around them. They looked like sardines sprinkled with the debris of the coach. It was as silent inside that car as a church sanctuary.

*Postscript:*

On July 31, 2005, Cuyahoga Falls civic officials and residents gathered on the 65th anniversary of the Doodlebug disaster for the formal dedication of a public memorial to its victims. The handsome black granite marker at 2641 Front Street lists the names of the dead and the survivors. Funds for the memorial and its landscaping were raised by seventh-grade students at Sill Middle School in Cuyahoga Falls. The Cuyahoga Falls Historical Society now maintains a "Doodlebug Journal" to which the public may contribute personal stories about the disaster and consult other accounts of the tragedy.

# "BREATH OF DEATH"

## The Cleveland Clinic Fire

## (1929)

Many disasters announce themselves with a bang. Most Cleveland catastrophes have done so literally. The 1944 East Ohio Gas fire began with an explosion that could be heard in Shaker Square and seen in Chagrin Falls. The 1932 Ellington Apartments inferno and the 1916 Waterworks tragedy likewise came with impressive blasts. And the 1908 S. S. Kresge fire started with probably the greatest fireworks display in Cleveland history.

Not so with the Cleveland Clinic disaster. It came, initially invisible and unknown, through the walls and pipe conduits of the Clinic building. It then announced itself indirectly to its victims as powdery flecks and puffs of smoke from heating vents and radiators. And many of its 123 dead may already have died when the first blast came at about 11:25 a.m., May 15, 1929.

Even then, as now, the Cleveland Clinic was one of the greatest success stories in Cleveland history. Founded in 1921, it was the joint medical dream of Doctors George W. Crile, Frank E. Bunts, and William E. Lowther. The three had served together in Cleveland's Lakeside Medical Unit in France during World War I, and had been much inspired by the model of team medical practice and technique the unit had perfected to treat the mass medical casualties of the Western Front. Joining with Dr. John Phillips and drawing on the model of the Mayo Clinic, the four doctors had, in only eight years, created a medical powerhouse that was known throughout the world. Already it was the pride of Cleveland, and celebrities, rulers of state, and thousands of more mundane folk came yearly to find comfort and cure at the hands of its skilled staff.

Although miniscule, compared to its present size, the 1929 Clinic was an impressive physical plant. Located just west of East 93rd on the south side of Euclid Avenue, the grounds included a 184-bed hospital and a research building used for special laboratories, such as X-rays. The main building, on the south side on Euclid Avenue at 93rd, was a four-story structure of reinforced concrete and brick. Used for both administration and diagnosis, its dozens of offices were employed by doctors for consultation and outpatient procedures.

It was to the main building—considered "fireproof" when built in 1920—that tragedy came on the morning of May 15, 1929. The bulk of the building's activities occurred in dozens of consulting rooms on the upper three floors. An interior court arched from the second floor up to a 30-foot-by-38-foot skylight at the roof. Two elevators and two staircases provided access to the three floors above, with offices off the mezzanine-style balconies that flanked the interior court.

Like most buildings of the era, the Main Clinic building's vital physical functions were centered and controlled from its basement. About a third of the area of the 75-foot-by-124-foot building, the basement included unused steam boilers (rendered unnecessary by the Clinic's new central heating plant), heating pipes, and storage rooms for files, supplies, and drugs. Fatally, it also contained a storage room for Clinic patients' X-rays.

Clinic chief Dr. George Crile would insist, in the wake of the disaster, that there was "no precedent" for the Clinic tragedy. That wasn't quite true, whether he knew it or not. In September 1923, gases generated from burning X-ray film and driven through a ventilating system had overwhelmed victims at a Syracuse hospital. And in Albany, in March 1928, eight persons had been killed

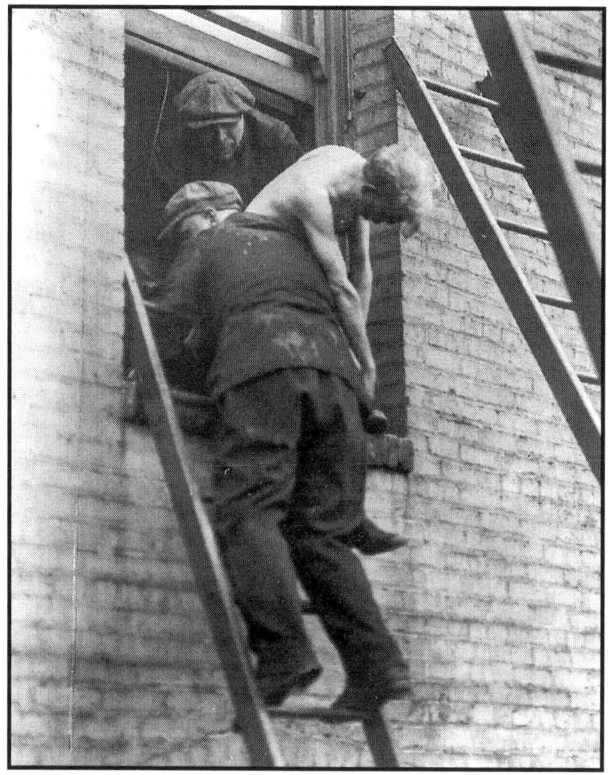

Victim being taken out of a Cleveland Clinic window, May 15, 1929.

when toxic fumes from burning X-rays had spread through another hospital.

The villain in both lethal accidents was nitrocellulose X-ray film, composed of camphor and a substance called pryoxylin (created by treating cotton with boiling nitric and sulfuric acids), with a very thin layer of gelatin added to make usable film. Usable—and very dangerous. It had already caused enough deaths and injuries by 1924 to warrant its replacement with a new acetate-based film marketed by Eastman Kodak that year.

Given its lethal contents, the Clinic's basement X-ray storage room was dangerous enough.The room contained about 70,000

X-ray sheets—at least 4,200 pounds of film, each pound capable of producing between 3 and 6 cubic feet of toxic gases. Several factors—most in violation of American Hospital Association guidelines—made the situation more dangerous. Unlike those in many other medical facilities, Clinic X-rays were not stored in metal containers. Although some were stored in metal filing cabinets, many films were filed in open wooden racks and all films were filed in flammable paper or manila folder jackets. Unlike many other large medical facilities, the Clinic had no fire sprinkling system in the storage room, nor in any other area of the building. And, going against an increasingly common practice in American hospitals, X-ray films were not stored in an area isolated from patient areas. Worst of all—almost unbelievably—the main Clinic building's ventilation system was also located in the X-ray storage room.

Like most terrible accidents, the Clinic tragedy was the cumulative product of mundane and individually innocuous circumstances. About January 1929, Miss Enid Critcher asked Clinic chief custodian Walter Adams to do something about the poor lighting in the X-ray storage room. Although the room was lit by four 100-watt drop fixtures, Critcher found it difficult to see in some areas of the room when she filed X-ray films. Adams responded by putting a "Y" double outlet at the end of one of the drop fixtures. Such an outlet could service either two 100-watt bulbs or one bulb and an electrical plug outlet. Adams would later deny that he even knew that an eight-foot extension cord was hooked up to a female end of that "Y" fixture. Or, as Miss Critcher testified, that it was connected to a 100-watt bulb "trouble light," which was strung over a "big spike" and hung down near the film cabinets. "I wouldn't do anything like that or I wouldn't allow it if I knew of it," Adams later insisted.

There was no inkling of the woe to come when a man with the improbably Dickensian name of Buffery Boggs arrived at the main Clinic building about 9 a.m. on May 15. A steamfitter's helper employed by the W. R. Rhoton Company, Boggs was there to repair a leaking steam pipe in the basement X-ray storage room. Water from the leak had already damaged some films, and the damaged ones had been removed from racks and placed away from the faulty pipe *on top of the storage cabinets* to prevent further damage.

Boggs got to work right away. Stripping away 14 inches of half-inch magnesia insulation, he quickly located the source of the leak. The pipe was too hot for patching work, though, so he went to the central power plant and requested that they shut the heat off. He then left the building. Before he departed, however, he took note of the improvised lighting that custodian Adams denied: "Just a common everyday light bulb dropped down on an extension cord from the ceiling."

Did Boggs smoke a cigarette or two while he was stripping that steampipe? Investigators of the Clinic disaster, especially a panel of lawyers hired by the Clinic to take sworn statements in its own probe, focused on the possibility that film combustion had been triggered by a cigarette left by Boggs in the X-ray room. All witnesses examined were queried as to their smoking habits, their observation of any smoking by anyone in the vicinity of the film room, and in particular, the smoking habits of one Buffery Boggs. Boggs admitted to a moderate smoking habit, but the official City investigation of the tragedy noted that during his testimony Boggs "appeared to be an incessant cigarette smoker." In retrospect, this would seem a gratuitous slur, as no physical evidence was ever produced to indicate that Boggs smoked in the X-ray film room on May 15.

Boggs returned to his task shortly after 11 a.m. As he walked through the door to the X-ray storage room he heard a "hissing sound." Although he didn't smell any odor, he noticed that "the room was warm, it was darn warm." He was beginning to wonder about the hissing—the steam had been turned off for more than an hour—when he saw the smoke. It was a "thick, yellowish smoke" coming from a steam line near the north wall. Boggs ran out of the room and yelled to Clinic maintenance worker Sam Steel for a fire extinguisher, "There's a fire in that room!" Steel handed a soda-ash extinguisher to Boggs, and Boggs ran back in the film room and began to spray the spreading cloud of yellowish-brown smoke.

It didn't help. Just about the time he emptied the extinguisher, Boggs was overcome by smoke and fell to the floor. "It stopped my breath, just as you would shut off a valve," was the way the steamfitter's helper put it. Coming to, he crawled toward the open door. As he reached it, a "gigantic force" picked him up and blew him through the door and across the floor on his stomach into a machine room. Boggs recalled, "It was as if a million cushions hit you at once."

Buffery Boggs's "gigantic force" was the disaster's first explosion and it came about 11:25 a.m. There were anywhere from 250 to 330 people in the building—and most of the day's 123 dead may already have been well on the way to the grave even before the first blast came. Decomposition (flameless combustion) or "cooking" of the X-ray films in the basement storage room, caused by heat, had apparently been going on for some time. By the moment of the initial explosion at 11:25 a.m., lethal gases had thoroughly penetrated both the piping and ventilation systems of the Clinic building right up to the roof. Bromine, nitrogen dioxide, nitrous oxide, nitrogen peroxide, hydrocyanic gas, hydrogen and oxygen gases—all released from the burning film—were being forced throughout all four floors of the building as fast as the ventilation ducts and piping chases could carry them. The first blast probably came when just enough of the free hydrogen in the walls came in contact with a convenient spark.

First hints that something was amiss in the Clinic came several minutes before the first explosion. Some employees and patients, especially women, noticed a peculiar, unpleasant odor in the air. H. W. Decker, Clinic pharmacist, was on the ground floor when he sensed the foul smell and found a group of nurses gathered by its apparent source in a radiator. Dorothy Hyde, a typist in the pharmacy, was oblivious to all but her typing—until "some fine powder, plaster or something" began falling on her work. About the same time, Mrs. H. A. Brooks saw some yellow dust coming out of a

Fire investigator in Cleveland Clinic X-ray film basement storage room.

hole in the wall and employee Maude Lehman became aware of a puff of smoke coming out of the wall. She had just told a staff doctor about it when the first blast shook the building, and choking clouds of dirty, yellow-brown smoke enveloped all four floors of the structure.

What went on in the Clinic building during the next 20 minutes is known only to God. Patterns of death, injury, and escape in the Clinic tragedy would later be pieced together, but events were really a maddened, incomprehensible chaos as at least 250 persons frantically sought to escape suffocating death in a suddenly gas-filled, burning concrete and wood trap. So lethal were the gases, especially the nitrogen peroxide and carbon monoxide, that most of the victims died probably within minutes of the first explosion, if not before. Patients died without a sound on examination tables. Doctors suddenly fell to the floor, scalpels still in hand. As Battalion Fire Chief Michael Graham later recalled of a corpse he found sitting in the second floor lobby: "He looked as if he had just started to take a nap when the fumes began." Others died screaming and crawling on the floors and window sills, gasping for air.

It was a particularly gruesome death, as many eyewitnesses would testify. Although the exact chemical components and proportions of the lethal gases were never determined, it is clear that large amounts of carbon monoxide and acidic nitrogen compounds were present. The effects on the lungs of the victims was rapid and lethal. Dr. Torald Sollmann, dean of the Western Reserve School of Medicine, described them clinically:

> In some way not known, the gas gets fixed in the thin walls of the lungs. The resulting irritation makes these cells soluble and as a result the watery part of the blood stream begins to leak through them into the lungs. The lungs fill with water, drowning the patient.

Not just drowning them, however: Coroner A. J. Pearse's report noted that "those who died from the poison gas bubbled at the nose and mouth." Witnesses testified that many of the faces of corpses appeared yellow, blue, and green.

An even more graphic description came from the vacationing Dr. William G. Epstein, who had unluckily stopped off in Cleveland—"on the spur of the moment"—with his wife, Florence. He was in another Clinic building when the first blast came, and he fought his way into the building to find:

> It was too horrible to describe. . . . That gas is awful stuff. It bites into the skin like acid—worse than acid. Because acid at least is localized. This gas eats into the tissues—and eats and eats and eats! . . . . Her mouth was bleeding—her eyes and nose were bleeding. She couldn't speak.

Florence Epstein died in her husband's arms. Dr. Howard Karsner of the Western Reserve Medical School stated that he had never, in a career of 20,000 autopsies, seen conditions identical to those of Clinic gas victims.

The situation was probably worst on the second and third floors. Most of the people in the building were with doctors and nurses in the dozens of examining and diagnostic rooms on those floors, and the poison gas and explosion caught some patients in various stages of undress. Virtually all doctors and nurses behaved heroically and began trying to take patients on these floors to safety. Unfortunately, most patients were strangers to the Clinic and their ideas of safety lay in the most obvious locations: the Clinic's stairways and elevators. This only increased their peril and panic, as intense fires were already raging at blowtorch heat in the rear elevator well and stairway. Lethal gases coming up from the basement, moreover, were concentrating in the three stories of the interior court—meaning that patients were safer staying in the side rooms and awaiting rescue via the windows.

Practically no one involved in the escalating disaster knew that. Which is why most of the victims were later found stacked—sometimes a dozen or more together—in piles by the staircases and the second- and third-floor elevator doors. So frantic was the press of desperate escapees by the third floor elevator that its metal doors were later found partially pushed in by the frenzied hands of desperate victims. Their hysteria was so great that a man in a wheelchair, caught in the wild panic, was later found with his feet jammed between the half-open door and the gaping elevator shaft. Coroner Pearse thought some died of sheer fright, and one panicked man jumped to his death from a fourth floor window.

Some escaped almost immediately from the spreading gas and fire. Custodian Walter Adams was the first person out of the building, his clothes aflame. Buffery Boggs, the unfortunate discoverer of the film fire, was blown by the second explosion into a window well in the Clinic's basement. He and a companion got themselves out of it, and Boggs—after prudently moving his car—ran all the way to the East 105th St. Fire Station and shouted, "There's a terrible fire at the Clinic, a big fire!"

The first alarm, probably preceding Boggs's announcement, was pulled at Fire Box #315 at 11:30 a.m. The Eighth Fire Battalion (Hook & Ladder Company #8, Engine Companies #10 & #22, and Rescue Squad #3), under Chief Michael Graham, roared out of the 105th Street Firehouse. They could smell and see the dense yellow-brown gas several blocks before they got to the burning building and they were already donning gas masks when they got there. By now, about 11:40 a.m., fires were raging in the film room, rear elevator, and rear stairwell, with six minor fires elsewhere in the building.

Fortunately for those trapped in the Clinic, rescue efforts had already spontaneously begun. A. W. Johnson and Roy Miller were up on 40-foot ladders painting a sign just west of the Clinic when the first blast occurred. Almost immediately afterwards, Johnson saw dense clouds of "umber" smoke (after all, he was a painter) pouring out of the building. He and Miller grabbed their ladders and ran with them to the west wall of the Clinic. There, joined by a young man named Walter Jackson, they ran the ladders up to the second-floor windows, where dozens of terrified people were screaming and even hanging onto the sills to avoid gas pouring out of the windows. Jackson, Miller, and Johnson, joined by Frank Salvini and Bruce Griffith from the nearby Hupmobile dealership at 93rd and Carnegie, climbed up the ladders and began to take frantic, often injured victims down, one by one. Except for Jackson, an unexpected and veritable Porthos when the chips were down on that fatal May day; one impressed witness later testified, "I saw him walk with two people down the ladder the same as you would go downstairs."

Incredibly, Walter Jackson performed even greater feats that terrible day. As the toxic gases and heat from the building often prevented rescuers from getting close enough to maneuver their ladders to the second-floor sills, Jackson actually held a ladder up with his hands and shoulders while rescuers carried bodies down it. John Smith, an eyewitness, never forgot the sight:

Ruins of 2nd floor lobby of Cleveland Clinic.

> I saw him hold up a ladder, full of people, with the strength God gave no human being. When he could stand that no longer he staggered to the side of victims on the ground, tearing off his shirt to wrap around a naked person.

Walter Jackson and his companions weren't the only heroes that day. Patrolman Ernest Staab was near the Clinic when the fire started and rushed into the building. He pulled 21 bodies out before he collapsed. Like many of the day's heroes who survived, he paid a price: he was subject to fainting spells for months after the accident. (And Staab proved to be a creature of heroic habit. Before he retired in 1954 he also rescued three children from the path of a drunken driver.)

One of the heroes was an anonymous man known only as "Jimmy" to William Majury, who described him to reporters. As the two men approached the burning Clinic, "Jimmy" said, "That looks like gas; I'm going in there." Majury watched as he ran in and emerged with a body, only to return to the blazing, smoking inferno.

Some heroes came in groups. One was composed of pupils from the Wilcox Commercial School on Euclid Avenue at East 100th. Against the orders of firemen at the scene, they entered the burning Clinic and began pulling victims out.

Eight doctors and six nurses died that day, and the evidence is that they all succumbed heroically, trying desperately to save their patients. One such was Dr. John Phillips, one of the four Clinic founders. Escaping from the Clinic, he worked outside for hours, treating the victims spread out on the grass. That evening, he collapsed at his apartment and died there, despite the frantic efforts of Dr. George Crile to save him. Another hero-doctor, albeit a survivor, was Dr. Wilson J. Peart, head of the Clinic's dental wing. Treating patients on the third floor when the initial explosion occurred, he shrewdly attempted to prevent them from going out into the hall adjacent to the interior court. Although his assistant and a technician got out of the room and died, Dr. Peart managed to drag several collapsed victims back into the room and to open windows. He and fellow physician Wallace Duncan refused to leave until firemen had rescued all 18 of the other people in the room.

William Brownlow, Clinic medical artist, died in dramatic and sublime fashion. He was in his third-floor studio and already succumbing to gas when Clinic usher Susan Brantweiner ran in. As he attempted to smash a window, she crawled across the floor to him and said, "Goodbye." Brownlow muttered, "No, not goodbye," shattered the window, grabbed Brantweiner and thrust her into the air outside. Firemen eventually rescued her, but Brownlow refused to go until two other victims had been removed from the room. He died soon after. Many patients would never forget the brave Clinic nurses shouting, "Save the patients, save the patients!" as death closed in.

Heroism did not know any age, much less sex or race that awful day. Perhaps the most astonishing sight of the disaster was 81-year-old Fire Chief George Wallace carrying on like a hero of youthful years. Among the first firemen at the scene, he pulled a victim from the elevator shaft and fell twice while rescuing others. All in a day's work, though, for the doughty Wallace, who served as an active Cleveland fireman from 1869 to 1931.

A second, and far more powerful, explosion occurred several minutes after the first firemen arrived on the scene. It was probably a blessing, as it blew out many remaining Clinic windows so that firemen could now see victims at windows that had been hidden by smoke. It also blew out the roof skylight and left several holes in the roof, thus ventilating much of the toxic gas in the three-story interior court. Within minutes, firemen had snaked their new 85-foot motorized ladder to the roof. Descending through the ruined skylight, Firemen Howard McAllister and Peter Rogers were lowered into the smoke- and gas-filled interior court. Swinging from side to side, they finally got inside the fourth-floor railing and began pulling victims, packed four deep in some places, out of the stairwell and elevator areas. They sent 15 victims to the roof, some dead, and some who were revived there by pulmotors. So many bodies were taken to the County Morgue that they had to lay them out on the floor for identification by stunned relatives and Clinic staff.

It was all over by 1:15 p.m., although a third explosion occurred shortly after the second. By that hour virtually all fire units on the East Side were on the scene. All victims had been removed and all fires were under control, except for a few smoldering window frames and part of the roof area. It was not over, however, for many of the victims. The lingering or delayed effects of the gas were potently manifested in the fact that some disaster victims quoted in initial newspaper accounts of the tragedy showed up in later editions as fatalities. Some fought death for hours, some for days, and one, attorney Henry Lustig, 47, battled until June 13, almost a month after the disaster. Accompanying his father-in-law to the Clinic, Lustig had tried in vain to save him when the first blast came and had stayed in the gas-filled building to aid several women trapped there. Although the official Clinic death toll was

100-watt light bulb suspected as probable cause of Cleveland Clinic fire.

123, lingering casualties such as Lustig may have swelled the actual total to 128.

If careless and casual in the procedures and conditions that produced the disaster, the Clinic and its human resources were magnificent in response and recovery. Dr. Crile himself was at his best throughout the disaster, a veritable battlefield general who tirelessly marshalled resources to heal the wounded and console the grieving. After hours tending the injured, Crile established a new Clinic headquarters across the street in the old Wason mansion (former site of Laurel School) and announced: "We must carry on. The Clinic has its work to do and must go forward."

As Clinic efforts to rebuild and recover went forward, so, too, did efforts to explain this unprecedented and ghastly accident. City, county, and state probes were under way within days of the disaster, supplemented by investigations by the War Department, Western Reserve University, the Bureau of Standards, and the National Board of Fire Underwriters. The results of these various inquiries are best summarized by noting that they held no one particularly or individually liable for the tragedy and that they agreed that the

Clinic disaster never should have happened, given existing knowledge about nitrocellulose film. Provoking much criticism, County Coroner A. J. Pearse's inquest was held in private, owing, Pearse said, to the reluctance of witnesses to testify in public. After lengthy sessions involving dozens of witnesses, Pearse concluded there was no need to call a Grand Jury to investigate or apportion blame for the mishap.

Probably the most thorough inquiry was the Clinic's own, undertaken by some of the best lawyers available in the city. Taking sworn statements from virtually all Clinic employees and disaster witnesses, they narrowed the disaster's origin down to three possibilities:

1. "spontaneous" combustion of the film, owing to overheating of the storage room;
2. film combustion caused by a carelessly left cigarette or match (hence the persistent inquiries about the smoking habits of Buffery Boggs);
3. film combustion caused by contact with the extension cord light dropped over the "big spike" near the film racks.

No one ever proved that Buffery Boggs or anyone else was smoking in the film room that day, although charwoman Rose Rebar testified that she often saw people smoking in the Clinic basement. And while Fire Warden J. H. Andrews had found a pack of cigarettes in the film room during his inspection *only five days before*—there was no tobacco evidence found to support the "careless smoker" theory. It is true that Boggs noted that the film room was "darn warm" on the morning of the fire, but the heat from the steam pipes hardly seemed sufficient to cause "cooking" of the X-ray films.

Which left the 100-watt bulb at the end of the spike-draped extension cord as the probable cause of the mishap. It was found in the ruins of the film storage room, and Enid Critcher testified that she had employed it for several months up to the day of the disaster. Custodian Walter Adams, for his part, adamantly insisted that it wasn't there:

> As for that light bulb extension, if it was there after the fire, ghosts must have placed it there. We took special pains that the 100-watt bulbs were not within three feet of the X-ray films.

Interestingly, Adams also denied the assertion of virtually all fire investigators that the fire door of the film room could not close on that fatal day, owing to an obstructing steam pipe:

> We closed it every night. It was left open in the daytime so the room would have the same temperature as the rest of the building.

On May 24, the *Plain Dealer* noted that one of the chief witnesses in the city probe of the Clinic disaster had made "false statements" and that "they concerned the lights in the basement room." But no one was ever legally charged with negligence or culpability in the Clinic tragedy.

The National Fire Protection Association was not so kind in its assessment. On June 12 it issued a report that blistered both the city and Clinic for sloppy practice in handling and regulating X-ray films:

> It is inconceivable that the conditions responsible for the Cleveland hospital disaster could have been permitted to exist even for a single day had the management or the inspection authorities appreciated the hazard. . . . The physical facts are well established. There was a large quantity of nitrocellulose X-ray film in the basement. It was stored in obvious violation of proper precautions for the keeping of this material of known dangerous property.

No expense or expertise was spared in trying to arrive at a scientific understanding of the Clinic disaster. Both the War Department and Western Reserve University School of Medicine conducted elaborate tests on mice and rabbits to determine the toxicity of the

Casualties being tended on ground, May 15, 1929.

probable gases involved. Mice exposed to burning of gas residue scrapings from the Clinic walls—there were copious yellow-brown stains throughout the building—died with convulsions within one to two minutes. Lesser concentrations, test reports said, merely caused "cyanosis dyspnea."

The official probes and harmless recriminations dragged on for some time. The Cleveland Clinic, however, had already put it all behind. The Cleveland powers-that-be, represented by an elite committee of Samuel Mather and 35 other similar achievers, rallied behind the Clinic, and Dr. George Crile impressively rebuilt it from the ruins of May 15, 1929. The main building was rebuilt on a different plan, to spare the sensibilities of those who might remember its appearance on that dreadful day. The massive insurance claims were paid off. And the Clinic has only waxed greater and more glorious as a Cleveland, indeed global, institution in the years since. It did, however, switch to acetate-based film and enforce some safety regulations and recommendations concerning X-ray film storage.

Why did the Clinic disaster happen? No one person was ever

held accountable, so it is now a moot point. But certain notes on the Clinic's fire inspections during the 1920s raise intriguing questions about municipal inspection procedures and enforcement. On May 4, 1925, for example, City Fire Warden J. H. Andrews inspected the film storage room and ordered the Clinic to keep its X-rays *in metal containers and to provide a fire-proof vault for same.* [Italics added.] This, obviously, was not done. Four months later, on September 15, 1929, Andrews noted, "This Company has not complied with my orders in regards to storing films [in metal cases]." There is no further record of violation or compliance. On May 10, 1929, Andrews made his last inspection and warned Clinic officials not to allow smoking in the film area. The inspection record makes no mention of a vault or metal cases at all.

# SOONER OR LATER...

## The Thompson Trophy Tragedy

## (1949)

In hindsight, it now seems like the inevitable accident. On September 5, 1949, during the annual National Air Races held at Cleveland Airport, a modified F-51 Mustang air racer crashed into a Berea home, killing the plane's pilot, a young mother, and her infant son. Even the *Plain Dealer*, which had never ventured a discouraging word about the Labor Day weekend event, opined solemnly, "What was bound to happen sooner or later in the National Air Races happened late Labor Day afternoon." Behind that phrase lies the untold tale of an accident that never should have happened.

The National Air Races were started in 1920 and lured to Cleveland in 1929 by the city's power elite (Alva Bradley, M. J. Van Sweringen, et al.). They soon became an annual ritual and emblem of Cleveland's pretensions to premier urban status. Held at Cleveland Airport, the races attracted enormous crowds, featured such aviation celebrities as Charles Lindbergh, James Doolittle, and Wiley Post, and garnered Cleveland coveted media attention throughout the world. Among the events were such crowd-pleasers as the cross-country Bendix Trophy race (a long-distance marathon from Los Angeles to Cleveland) and the daredevil Thompson Trophy contest (a closed-course, high-speed race around pylons), ensuring that the National Air Races became a fixed institution in Northeast Ohio—despite their real dangers to both pilots and civilians. Dangers that increased every year, as the aircraft got faster, the crowds waxed greater, and—in retrospect the most obviously ignored element—the once exurban region surrounding the Cleveland Airport became suburbanized, with ever-growing housing subdivisions. By the late 1930s, indeed, it is fair to say that it was not a question of whether a terrible tragedy was going to occur, but when.

The death toll began at the very first races held here in 1929. Five pilots were killed in cross-country flying accidents away from the Cleveland area. Locally, pilot Thomas Reid was killed on August 31 when his big green Emsco aircraft crashed in the woods near West 226th Street and Westwood Road, just three hours after he set a new world record for solo endurance flight. Other lowlights of the 1929 event were the crash of Lady Mary Heath's Great Lakes Trainer through the roof of the Mills Company at 965 Wayside Drive, and the near death of parachutist Norma Stevens when her chute failed to open properly in an abrupt descent on Grayton Road.

The mayhem resumed on September 3, 1934, when Douglas Davis, the winner of that year's Bendix race, lost control of his plane during the eighth lap of the Thompson Trophy race, a high-speed course with tight turns plotted at low altitudes over the suburbs ringing Cleveland Airport. Just as Davis negotiated the number two pylon, his black-and-white monoplane shot straight up into the air—and then straight down at a speed of at least 350 miles per hour. Seconds later, the plane smashed into a field in North Olmsted Village near Lorain and Gessner Roads. Efforts to extricate Davis's pulverized corpse were hampered by thousands of Clevelanders who thronged the scene trying to scavenge souvenirs from the grisly wreckage.

The next fatality came at 6:50 p.m. on September 2, 1937, when the wings of pilot Lee Miles's Miles-Atwood Special disintegrated during speed trials at the airport. Miles was killed instantly when his fuselage slammed into some woods on the property of John C. Fischer at 4950 Grayton Road. The tragedy was almost repeated the next day when Count Otto von Hagenburg of Germany, a celebrated stunt flyer, crashed while performing a routine that put his plane upside down at an altitude of one foot—while doing 150 miles per hour.

Amazingly, Hagenburg walked jauntily away from his broken plane with only a slight head wound and a wave to the stunned crowd.

The deadly pace of these airborne disasters accelerated in 1938. During a qualifying trial on August 31, the engine of Russell G. Chambers's plane exploded at an altitude of 150 feet. Crashing into Will Thomson's pear orchard between Wagar and Clague Roads in Rocky River, Chambers died several days later from a fractured skull. Three days after his crash, a connecting rod in George Dory's fleet Bushy-McGrew racer broke while he was flying in the Greve Trophy Race. The courageous Dory managed to maneuver his plummeting plane through a crowded residential area before it crashed into the dead end of West 227th Street, about one-third of a mile north of Lorain. The badly injured Dory was pulled from his smashed craft by an eight-year-old boy and his father. Everyone marveled at how "lucky" it was that his plane had not hit someone's home.

The 1939 races, the last held before the end of the coming war, brought more of the same. On September 3, some 65,000 spectators saw Leland Williams's red Brown Racer spin out of control and smash into a field on the farm of Charles Nock between Rocky River Drive and Grayton Road. Williams was killed instantly, but the mess was soon cleaned up and the usual lack of thought given to the potential carnage to come.

If success is measured by attendance, the 1947 races were the best ever, with several hundred thousand spectators jamming the three-day event. But there was no letup in the violence, which began even before the formal events commenced. On August 25 pilot James C. DeSanto bailed out of his Curtiss P-60E aircraft after watching his elevator and tail fall off the plane during a test sprint. He landed safely, suffering only minor bruises, but his plane crashed into a corn patch owned by Fred Techmyer on Hummel

Road in Brook Park. The following day pilot Claude Smith also parachuted to safety after something in the left wing of his Falcon Special snapped and he careened toward the ground. He landed in a field off Eastland Road some seconds after his plane slammed into a lot on Eastland, just 150 feet from the home of W. A. Waddups. Four days later James C. Ruble, an entrant in the cross-country Bendix race, bailed out of his burning P-38 Lightning fighter over the Arizona desert after his engine caught fire. No one was hurt in that mishap either, but the worst was yet to come.

It came during the Thompson Trophy race on September 1, aptly described by the *Plain Dealer* as "the wildest, fastest 30 minutes of air racing in history." While 75,000 spectators goggled, Clevelander Anthony R. Jannazo lost control of his navy surplus Corsair and plunged into a field on Royalton Road, near Marks Road in Strongsville. As his plane exploded, hurling Jannazo's body clear, the Corsair's engine skipped across Royalton Road, narrowly missing a car with four persons in it, knocked down three apple trees, and buried itself in the ground. Minutes later, J. L. Ziegler bailed out of his P-40 fighter after his engine failed, landing in a patch of swamp off Brookpark Road and breaking his right leg. His plane continued on, a wing slicing off the top of a boxcar in the New York Central yard near West 150th Street and the fuselage crashing into an adjacent mesh of railroad tracks. About the same moment, Mrs. Melvin Patrick was hit and injured by Ziegler's Plexiglas cockpit cover, which landed on her while she was watching the air races from a chair in her yard at 5100 West 148th Street.

And there was still more destruction before the end of the 1947 races. Woodrow Edmondson was just rounding pylon number three when the engine of his P-51 Mustang exploded. Instead of bailing out, he tried landing it on the farm of H. M. Jacobs near Albion and Webster Roads. Edmondson was badly injured when his plane skidded into a grove of trees and caught fire. Meanwhile, another Thompson racer, Jack B. Hardwick, walked away from the crash landing of his P-51 with only a bruised elbow. After his engine failed early in the race he succeeded in bringing his plane down in

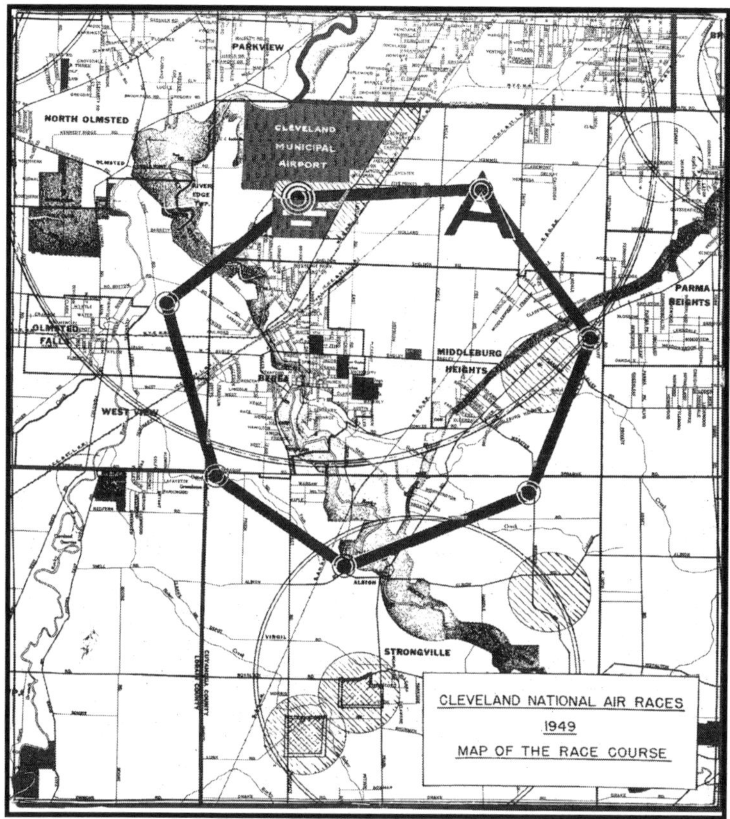


Map of the Thompson Trophy Race, National Air Races, 1949.

an empty field off Rocky River Drive in Brook Park. The races were getting bloodier by the year, and no one seemed to be counting the cost.

The year 1948 may have lured National Air Races officials into a false sense of security. There was but one fatality, and it could have been much worse. Midget plane racer Paul A. DeBlois was piloting his Bee Gee Baby Sportster through tests for the next day's Goodyear elimination race when his tiny plane literally began falling to pieces in the air over Cleveland Airport. Seconds later DeBlois was killed when his plane crashed into a gravel beach in the Rocky River

Reservation of the Metropolitan Park, several hundred feet north of the Brookpark Road bridge in Parkview Village. But that was mere anticlimax to the carnage of '47, so the debris were once again scraped up and preparations made for the 1949 races.

William P. Odum was a seemingly experienced, popular flier. Flying thousands of hours for the Royal Canadian Air Force during World War II, he quickly became a star on the competitive air race circuit after the war. Then, in 1947, he vaulted to worldwide fame by breaking Howard Hughes's 1938 record for round-the-world flight. An affable, charming 29-year-old, Odum was a favorite with fans of the National Air Races, both for his aeronautic feats and his personable manner. But after the tragedy that took his life and the lives of a Berea mother and her son, his piloting peers agreed that he should never have been at the controls of the death plane, a souped-up F-51 Mustang fighter.

To begin with, Odum had no experience in the *Beguine,* the plane loaned to him by celebrity flier Jacqueline Cochran. Secondly, he had never flown in any closed-course pylon competition, much less the Thompson Trophy race. Thirdly, the *Beguine* was designed to fly on a four-pylon course, not the seven-pylon Thompson. Cook Cleland, famed Cleveland flier who competed with Odum in the fatal race, put it this way after the tragedy:

> [I] don't think he should have been in the Thompson Trophy race at all. Not only I but some of the other pilots will tell you the same thing. He was a Bendix (the cross-country speed dash) pilot, not a closed course speed pilot. It takes two different kinds of temperament. Odum made an excellent cross-country flyer but I guess the ship he flew today was just too much for him.

It seems that Odum himself agreed with his peers, although he was quoted too late to spare himself and his victims. He told one of his fellow pilots, "I don't belong in this thing—I'm used to flying high off the ground." But none of these misgivings was publicly articulated by anyone as Odum arrived in Cleveland to compete in

Jeanne Laird, killed in her house.

the 1949 races, much less after he won the closed-course Sohio race with a record speed on Saturday, September 5.

With nine other Thompson contestants, Odum took off in his dark green racer at exactly 4:45 p.m. The end of the high-speed race's first lap, following a course laid out around seven pylons, found Odum in third place. Rounding the number one pylon near the airport, he headed southwest at a speed in excess of 400 miles per hour.

It happened as he passed the number two pylon, situated at Lewis and No Bottom Roads in Olmsted Township. Perhaps attempting to overcompensate for a wide turn, Odum turned his plane 60 degrees, instead of the expected 35 or 40. Then, as he tried to bank the plane back on course, the F-51 flipped over on its back and sped directly toward a brand-new residential neighborhood at West and Beeler Roads in Berea.

As Bradley Laird later put it, his "whole world ended" in just seconds of fire. At exactly 4:48 p.m. he was standing outside the $16,000 ranch house at 429 West Street that he and his wife Jeanne had just moved into on August 31. The 36-year-old stationery salesman was washing the outside windows of the house and having a playful water fight with his five-year-old son Bradley David. In the front yard was his father-in-law Benjamin Hoffman, 56, who was watching Laird's 13-month-old son Craig cavort in an adjacent playpen. It was a happy domestic scene, completed by the presence of Jeanne Laird, 24, who was watching her family and keeping half an eye on the air races through the bathroom window.

C. V. Talbot, one of the Lairds' neighbors, saw the crash. He was watching the planes in the air when he heard someone say, "Look, there's one of the planes off its course. It's coming right here." A second later, Talbot saw a streak of silver light, as the plane careened over his house top. Another second later, he heard a soft "ploosh" as the plane hit the Lairds' attached garage and the nearly full gas tanks inside ignited.

Odum's F-51 Mustang hit the Laird house so hard and fast that it bored through the concrete foundation and buried its nose six feet into the earth underneath. Odum was killed instantly and incinerated so completely that rescuers found little more than his watch when they finally found his remains four feet down. Jeanne Laird probably also perished fairly quickly. She was trapped in the bathroom as the house was enveloped in the gas-fed flames and could not have survived long.

The hero of the disaster was Benjamin Hoffman. Stunned by the impact of the plane and the ensuing fire, he turned to see his 13-month-old grandson Craig in flames in his playpen. Grabbing the child, he ran into the street, frantically tearing the burning clothes off the baby and screaming "Save the children! Save the children!" to neighbors as they rushed to give aid. Even after he was put in an ambulance, Ben Hoffman broke away three times to try to save his daughter from the blazing house.

It was too late. Bradley Laird had already tried to rescue his

**Odom Crash Hero Haunted by Failure to Save "Babies"**

September 9, 1949.

trapped wife several times but had been driven away by the flames. He was lucky to save his son Bradley David, who escaped unhurt. There was little for Berea firemen to do when they arrived at the site except to put out the fire and help the neighbors carry furniture out of the house and onto the lawn. Ben Hoffman survived his ordeal with burns on his head and hands. Baby Craig was not so lucky, dying at Berea Community Hospital three hours after the fire from burns over 80 percent of his tiny body.

The aftermath of the disaster was what Clevelanders had come to expect from such affairs. Bradley Laird took his family back to Minneapolis. Insurance companies, including Lloyd's of London, paid off the accident claims against Odum's estate and the National Air Races. Led by anguished and outraged Berea citizens, a number of affected suburbs quickly passed ordinances banning closed-course air racing in their civic air space.

And the National Races disappeared from Cleveland until 1964, when they were reborn at Burke Lakefront Airport in the much tamer, safer format in which they continue to the present. Few people, especially those civic officials and elite citizens who had brought the races to Cleveland, ever admitted that what had occurred was bound to happen, given the careless negligence with which they had conducted the prestigious event.

# BURNING, BURNING, BURNING RIVER

## The Cuyahoga River Fires (1868, 1912, 1922, 1952, 1969...)

June 22, 1969. Few Clevelanders would quibble with the designation of this milestone as Cleveland's undisputed day of infamy. For that was the day the Cuyahoga River caught fire, and soon thereafter Cleveland spontaneously combusted as a national laughingstock and byword for urban dysfunction. The received wisdom about that infamous blaze is that it signaled the nadir of the river's viability and ignited a sleeping citizenry to repair its badly compromised environment. True on both counts, in a general way, but there's much more to the burning Cuyahoga story than those simple facts. Sadly, like so many Cleveland stories, the full truth is much worse than you've been led to believe.

Nineteenth-century Clevelanders, like most Americans in the pre-*Silent Spring* epoch, paid little mind to the pollutants and poisons they dumped into their water supply. They did mind—and often complained about—the taste and smell of Cleveland water, which along with cholera and typhoid germs, carried the taste and odor of the petroleum refining refuse that John D. Rockefeller et al. were blithely pouring into Kingsbury Run, the Cuyahoga River, and

GASOLINE FIRE KILLS FIVE CAUGHT IN TRAP AT WORK

Fluid Leaking From Barge Being Filled, and Covering River, Bursts Into Flames Fatal to Mechanics Repairing Boat.

Three Companions of Victims Make Sensational Escape Through Blaze While Firemen Battle Against Explosions.

Five Tugs, Three Drydocks and One Yacht Are Ruined in Spectacle, While Standard Oil Boat Almost Escapes.

The *Plain Dealer*, May 2, 1912.

Lake Erie. Rather than forbidding such uncivil practices, however, they coped with oily water by building the city's water intake cribs farther and farther out in Lake Erie—as the bloody history of water crib accidents attests. (See the title story of *They Died Crawling* for a chronicle of those melancholy events.)

The first serious hint that Clevelanders would be paying escalating costs for their indifference to the environment came on August 29, 1868. Waste oil floating near the Seneca Street (West 3rd) bridge on the Cuyahoga ignited a wide area and came close to burning down a dense strip of industrial firms on the river's east side. Despite some subsequent, if mild, suggestions that the unlimited discharge of oil waste into the river be curbed, nothing was done. Fifteen years later, in 1883, such persistent disregard earned its due reward when a raging oil fire on the surface of Kingsbury Run (by now containing more oil than water) came within seconds of burning down the entire city. (See the chapter "Cleveland's Burning!".) More hands were publicly wrung, more suggestions for

CLEVELAND, THURSDAY, MAY 2, 1912.

PRICE ONE C

SCENES AFTER EXPLOSION OF OIL BARGE THAT KILLED FIVE MEN; FOUR OF VICTIMS

STANDARD OIL BARGE 88 ON WHICH EXPLOSION OCCURRED

LOUIS GALE

WHERE VICTIMS WERE TRAPPED UNDER BARGE

CARRYING OUT the BODIES of the DEAD

1912 Cuyahoga River fire. *Cleveland Leader*, May 2, 1912.

industrial waste regulation were offered—and the contamination of the Cuyahoga River by flammable liquids continued unabated. Despite another scare in August of 1887, when a grain elevator fire ignited part of the river, the turn of the century found the Cuyahoga River chronically and visibly tainted with petroleum products. The problem was generally worse during the long Cleveland winters, when blockage by lake ice in the harbor further retarded the normally sluggish flushing action of the river.

The accident waiting to happen occurred May 1, 1912, at a Standard Oil cargo slip just south of the Jefferson Avenue bridge. Stan-

WHERE FIRE THREATENS FLAT WAREHOUSES

The 1930 Cuyahoga River fire. *Cleveland Press*, April 2, 1930.

dard Oil barge No. 8, containing 100,000 gallons of oil and naphtha, was being offloaded just across the river from the Great Lakes Towing Company's dry docks. Gasoline from No. 8 had been leaking into the river for some time, unbeknownst to anyone, when a spark from the passing tugboat *Superior* set off the first of six explosions at 3 p.m. Within seconds, oil and gasoline in the water likewise ignited, and an area of several hundred yards was inundated with flaming gasoline. By the time the fire was put out three hours later, it had incinerated five men, injured five others, destroyed five tugboats and three dry docks, and done additional damage to Great Lakes Towing. The dead men, working there as caulkers, had been trapped immediately between the dry dock flooring and the scow they were repairing. In the anguished civic postmortem, the *Plain Dealer* called for the flow of oil into the river to be curtailed but discreetly refrained from mentioning how it had gotten there in the first place. Cleveland fire chief George A. Wallace was, characteristically, more blunt. He stated that copious oil seepage from the Standard Oil works was the chief culprit and demanded that it be

The Cuyahoga River in flames, Jefferson Avenue bridge, November 1, 1952.

stopped. Cleveland city councilmen called for public hearings on the matter . . . and that, predictably, was the last heard about the riverine oil peril for some years.

Just 10 years later, on October 29, 1922, the 1912 disaster repeated itself, albeit with less lethal consequences. A fire of unknown origin broke out without warning at noon at the Great Lakes Towing Company's river docks on Jefferson Avenue. Although the blaze was contained within three hours, it damaged a lighter, a derrick, and a tugboat and for a while threatened the Jefferson Avenue bridge. Apparently, nothing was learned from the incident, as a similar blaze broke out in the Cincinnati slip of the Cuyahoga on April 2, 1930. This time the cause was a film of alcohol and oil in the slip, supposedly ignited by smoldering debris from the Cleveland Grain Elevator fire some three months previous. Although there was no serious damage, safety forces got a bad scare as billowing clouds of ominous smoke blanketed downtown.

By the 1940s, public hand-wringing about the growing flammability of the Cuyahoga had become so chronic as to be comically repetitive. One year the *Cleveland Press* would caution: "Experienced [firemen] see the oil-covered river as the starting place for a conflagration which might easily sweep a large portion of the city." The next year would furnish the warning that an oil boat "could cause a lot of damage to...[a] vessel; fire under a railroad bridge would put the operating machinery out of commission." But not even a serious oil blaze that warped the plates of the ore carrier *Negaunee* in March 1941 motivated city officials to significant action. Nor was any decisive cleanup action taken after an intense petroleum fire almost took out the Clark Avenue bridge on February 7, 1948, and caused $100,000 in damage. Nor were any additional reforms initiated after a leaking Cities Service Oil tank spewed thousands of gallons of gasoline into the river on May 16 of the same year. Cleveland officials did, however, step up their public rhetoric—a crescendo of dire warnings that climaxed with Fire Prevention Bureau chief Bernard W. Mulcahy's tough talk in May 1952. Citing "definite proof" that Standard Oil was responsible for a two-inch oil slick under the Jefferson Avenue bridge, Mulcahy thundered that he would have Standard Oil officials arrested if they failed to alleviate the problem.

Apparently, Standard Oil officials did fail, as the worst river fire in Cleveland history broke out only six months later at that very site. The first alarm went in at 2:16 p.m. on November 1, and by the time firemen arrived at the scene, flames were roaring through the Great Lakes Towing Company's dock area, climbing the Jefferson Avenue bridge, and heading fast for Standard Oil Refinery No. 1. Before the flames could be extinguished, the conflagration became a five-alarm fire, injuring one fireman and wreaking damage amounting to $1 million. One tugboat was ruined, two more were badly damaged, a workshop was destroyed, two dry docks were ruined, and the Jefferson Avenue bridge was put out of commission with charred flooring and a damaged lift mechanism.

The postmortems on the 1952 fire followed the familiar pat-

**Thick Coating of Oily Goo Lies on Cuyahoga River**

*Cleveland Press*, December 19, 1961.

tern. Chief Mulcahy brandished photographs taken several months before the fire showing six inches of oil on the surface of the water. Mulcahy further noted that the greatest potential danger point was where Kingsbury Run emptied into the river near Great Lakes Towing—the exact locus of the catastrophic 1883 oil fire. And the Cleveland Chamber of Commerce demanded that Mayor Thomas A. Burke take steps to eliminate the danger of fire posed by the Cuyahoga.

Meanwhile, river traffic resumed, the bridge was eventually repaired after a month . . . and oil and kindred fluids continued to pour unimpeded into Cleveland's crooked river.

Given this 100-year-plus back story of inflammable pollutants and ensuing, periodic riverine infernos, it may seem surprising that the 1969 Cuyahoga fire did not come as a mere anticlimax. By the standards of 1912 or 1952, it was a very modest mishap. On the morning of June 22 an oil slick floating under two wooden railroad trestles at the foot of Campbell Road caught fire. Reported at 11:56 a.m., the five-story-high flames had been put out by 12:20 p.m., as firemen operating from shore and from a fireboat quickly responded to the alarm. The cause of the fire—aside from the perilous insanity of allowing industries to dump heavy concentrations of oil on the water—was never determined. The total physical damage wrought by the blaze amounted to only $50,000, most of it suffered by the Norfolk and Western double-track trestle, the single-line Newburgh & South Shore viaduct incurring only slight damage. The damage to the city's reputation, however, was almost incalculable. Only two days after the conflagration, the *Plain Dealer* cited the fire as a provocation for nationwide mirth at Cleveland's expense: "Cleveland, eh? Isn't that the place where the river is so polluted it's a fire hazard? Yuk, yuk, yuk."

It wasn't funny to Clevelanders then, and it remains a festering wound in the civic psyche, forever aggravated by the sound of Randy Newman's jeering commemorative anthem, "Burn On." Forest City residents, however, should be grateful to Newman and others who made the last Cuyahoga River fire a pretext for mortifying civic abuse. Given the apathy and abuse that had produced a century of river fires, only such national scorn was able to spark the resurrection of the Cuyahoga River in the years since.

# DEATH IN THE DEEP PIT

## The Terminal Tower Tragedy

## (1928)

As Clevelanders we walk and motor through a death-drenched landscape. Progress never comes without a human price, and it is impossible to find a block in Greater Cleveland that does not have a tale of suffering and death somewhere in its history. (If you disbelieve that assertion, you might try one of the author's occasional trolley tours of Cleveland murder/disaster sites.) The construction of all the high-level bridges linking the East and West sides involved accidental deaths and injuries, from the genesis of the Superior Viaduct in the 1870s to the completion of the Main Avenue bridge in 1939. The erection of Cleveland's signature buildings, too, exacted their toll of dead and maimed, especially such illustrious structures as the Old Arcade, the Scofield Building, and the first Hollenden Hotel. But there is no more celebrated structure in Cleveland than the Terminal Tower—and it is therefore fitting that it was the site of the most sensational and poignant construction accident in Forest City history: the unintended concrete burial that took the lives of Patrick Toolis and Patrick Cleary.

It was, perhaps, inevitable, that some lives would be consumed in a project as large as the epic Terminal construction. It lasted seven years from groundbreaking to completion, requiring the razing of over a thousand existing structures. A mini-city of via-

Southwest corner of the Terminal Tower excavation, October 13, 1926.

ducts was created to support the network of streets (Ontario and Prospect for starters) that bounded the 52-story Union Terminal and its department store/hotel adjuncts. Much of the most dangerous toil involved the deep excavations for the Terminal, especially the 200-foot-plus borings down to the bedrock that supported the massive tower. Someone was going to get hurt sooner or later, and with record levels of cheap immigrant labor, it was likely to be sooner.

An ominous harbinger of the 1928 tragedy came without warning at noon on June 9, 1926. Several men laboring in a concrete well 192 feet deep had just returned to the surface at Ontario when the entire Public Square area was shaken by a powerful explosion originating in the well. The force of the blast knocked down workers within a 200-foot radius of the well. The central downtown area was filled with noxious smoke. There were no fatalities, although eight injured men were taken to the hospital as thousands of curious onlookers surged against police lines for a better look at the damage. It was later surmised that one of the returning workmen

Desperate rescuers at the top of the Terminal death pit, October 17, 1928

had lit a cigarette just as the elevator brought him to the surface, igniting a seam of methane gas that his crew had discovered below only minutes before. The wreckage was swept up, the gas pumped out, and the enormous project ground on.

October 16, 1928, was a pleasant autumn day. It was already dark at 7:30 p.m. as dozens of men toiled like so many purposeful ants in the vast acreage of the Terminal excavation. Much of their effort was devoted to digging deep shafts for the massive pillars supporting the viaduct of the rerouted Prospect Avenue running between Ontario Street and Superior behind the rising Terminal Tower. (Cleveland folklore has it that the depth of the Terminal support shafts was mandated by the presence of "quicksand" in the area; it was not quicksand but rather varying levels of more or less wet clay.) Seventy of the shafts had already been poured without incident, so there was no reason for laborers Patrick Toolis, 29, and Patrick Cleary, 27, to be alarmed. True, they were at the bottom of their pit, 103 feet below the future junction of Prospect and Superior Avenue. But there was enough air to breathe for their sched-

*Cleveland News*, October 17, 1928.

uled stint, and they were just rounding out the bell-shaped bottom of the shaft with their shovels so that its concrete fill could begin and they could move on to another shaft.

Like most workplace accidents, theirs happened with sickening suddenness. An identical 103-foot shaft next to the one holding Toolis and Cleary was in the process of being filled with liquid concrete. All that lay between the two shafts was the lining of their own shaft, four feet of earth (which narrowed to two feet at the bottom), and the second shaft lining. As protection, it wasn't enough. At about 7:30 p.m., 150 tons of liquid concrete from the second shaft burst through its lining, drove through two feet of dirt, smashed through the second lining, and began pouring onto the stunned Cleary and Toolis. There was one startled cry from the bottom, heard by a man on a scaffold higher up in the shaft . . . and then nothing but ominous silence as the streaming concrete found its equilibrium, settled . . . and began to harden.

Reaction was instantaneous at the top of the dig. Cleary and Toolis's fellow workers rushed to the shaft and began descending, buckets in hand, in shifts of three. It was cramped and claustrophobic 60 feet down in the shaft where they were working, which was only six feet in diameter, and there were at least 40 feet of rapidly hardening concrete on top of Toolis and Cleary. But the work went on desperately all that night and into the day as word of the disaster spread and more and more workers arrived to lend a hand to rescue efforts. Deeper and deeper they penetrated, boring inch by inch, first with buckets, then with chisels, and finally with pneumatic drills as the concrete firmed to rocklike hardness. Frantic efforts to maneuver a steam shovel into place to speed up the concrete removal proved fruitless due to the terrain and mechanical congestion of the Terminal excavation.

Even the most optimistic of the rescuers must have known how it would end. (In fact, Toolis and Cleary probably died from suffocation within 15 minutes at the most.) Although unencumbered by 100 tons of concrete, the rescuers themselves could barely breathe in the thin, methane-contaminated air near the shaft bottom, and the digging crews were soon rotating in 15-minute, and then 10-minute, shifts as exhausted rescuers came gasping back to the top. Finally, after 15 hours of digging, the arm, then the head, and finally the torso of Patrick Toolis appeared. His cement-encrusted body was found hurled against the side of the shaft where the flood of concrete caught him. Toolis's brothers Edward and John and his sister Rita were among those who stared as his stiff corpse was finally unloaded topside. As the Reverend Lawrence Ahearn of St. Ignatius of Antioch Roman Catholic Church administered the last rites, Rita Toolis—who had to be physically restrained from joining the rescuers in the shaft—was led away sobbing from the terrible scene. Patrick was soon reburied, this time in a plot at Calvary Cemetery.

About an hour later, Patrick Cleary's body was uncovered. When the men found him he was standing upright in the shaft bottom, his right hand stretched upward, only inches away from a ring-bolt on a hoist that would have carried him to safety. He had been on the job for only three days when death took him for its own.

The aftermath of the Terminal shaft tragedy was the sour denouement typical of a Cleveland disaster. The first investigating

*Cleveland Press*, October 17, 1928.

official on the scene, Cleveland police sergeant William F. Moralevitz, filed a report after interviewing eyewitnesses and workers at the project. His report concluded that Toolis and Cleary had been innocent of any negligence and that the shaft collapse was due to faulty construction and bad judgment on the part of the project engineer used by the contractor, the firm of Spencer, White and Prentiss.

Spencer, White and Prentiss, unsurprisingly, conducted their own investigation, and more unsurprisingly still, insisted that the accident was "unavoidable" and probably caused by the unforeseen collapse of an undetected vein of sand.

The city of Cleveland, for its part, maintained its historically casual laissez faire attitude to such industrial/construction catastrophes. When asked whether the city should have insisted on a greater distance between the two shafts, city building commissioner William D. Guion sniffed, "That lies entirely with the engineers. We do not concern ourselves with such construction problems."

Such was not the opinion of Ohio deputy factory and building inspector J. P. Cummings, who noted that the accident could have been avoided if only the construction engineers had waited for the cement in the first shaft to harden before preparing the second. So ended a ghastly chapter in the painful record of those who really built the Cleveland we know today—except for the lawsuits and the $6,500 each awarded to the Toolis and Cleary families.

# "THEY DIED CRAWLING"

## The Waterworks Tunnel Explosion (1916)

Water. If there is anything that Clevelanders take for granted, it is water. If we think of it at all, the image of Lake Erie's limitless gallons presents itself—and we leave it at that. Yes, we know that the water has to be pumped from the lake, treated with potent chemicals to make it safe, and then sent forth to gush out of our faucets. The historical truth about Cleveland's water supply, however, is a tale of disaster and death, terror and pain, and the seemingly expendable lives of the city's once enormous working-class population. Above all, it is the terrible story of Crib #5 and the events of July 24 and 25, 1916.

Water was no problem for Cleveland's pioneer residents. They took what they needed from Lake Erie and the Cuyahoga River and fretted far more about malarial fevers than water quality, barring the occasional outbreak of cholera. By 1856, however, Cleveland's lakeside water was visibly filthy, and so Cleveland's waterworks was begun with the laying of a 300-foot-long cast-iron pipe, 4 feet in diameter, extending out from the Old River Bed to a depth of 12 feet. The water was pumped to the city's first reservoir at Kentucky and Franklin streets; the elevated promenade atop the Kentucky Reservoir was long considered one of Cleveland's finest views.

By the 1870s, however, more clean water was needed to supply Cleveland's exploding population and thirsty industries and so a tunnel was dug from an intake crib 9,000 feet from shore to the pumping station on Division Avenue. Foreshadowing the unhappy future of the Cleveland waterworks, it cost the lives of 19 men; the first two died while investigating a gas smell by lighting a match. A second, parallel tunnel, however, was completed in May of 1890 without loss of life. Up until almost the turn of the century, most tunnel construction fatalities resulted either from cave-ins or "the bends," that awful complication particular to those who work underground in pressurized conditions.

The modern era of Cleveland water began on May 11, 1898, when tunnelers digging 6,300 feet offshore toward the Kirtland pumping station at East 49th hit a natural gas pocket. It exploded, burning eight of the tunnelers (or "sandhogs," as they called themselves). The eight burned men somehow managed to crawl 2,000 feet back up the tunnel towards shore, where fellow workers dragged them to safety. All eight men, however, subsequently died of their burns.

Exactly two months later, on July 11, 1898, the tragedy repeated itself when 11 sandhogs died as the same tunnel exploded again. After this disaster the tunnel was sealed off with a bulkhead, and workers began to burrow toward shore from two new cribs. On the night of August 14, 1901, one of the cribs caught fire, burning five men to death and drowning another five who jumped into the lake to escape the flames. Almost a week went by. Six days after the fire, Gustaf Van Duzen, a veteran sandhog, was repairing the burned crib when he heard tapping noises coming from the wrecked crib shaft. He and another man went down the shaft and found the exhausted and nearly starved miners Adam Kent and John Eugine. They had miraculously survived the fire but had been too weak and woozy from gas to climb out of the tunnel. This episode was but one chapter in the legend of heroism that grew up around Gus Van Duzen. We shall meet him again in this story.

The day after Van Duzen rescued the two miners, another gas explosion in the other new tunnel at Crib #3 destroyed the shaft, killing six men and flooding the works. Several survivors managed

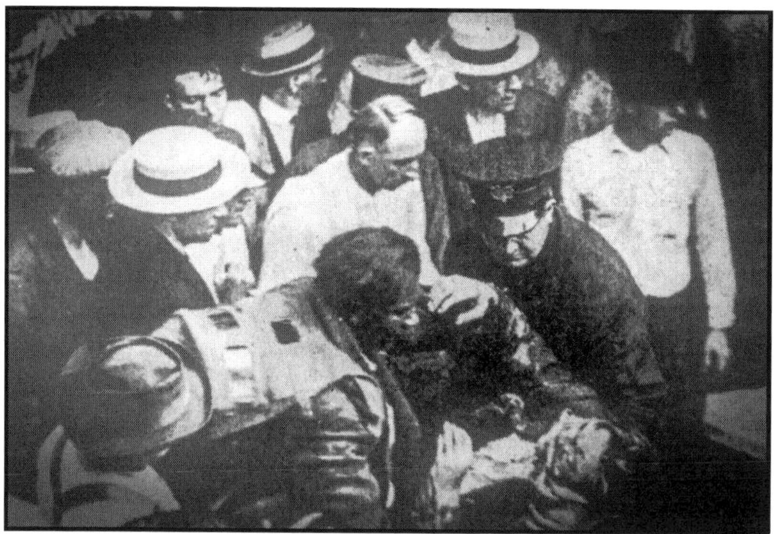

Garrett Morgan and rescued victim, July 25, 1916.

to cling to the crib ruins until they were rescued the next day. And yet another gas explosion the following year in the same tunnel killed four more sandhogs on December 14, 1902.

In all, probably 70 men lost their lives in tunnel operations before the fatal night of July 24, 1916. It was not a proud record, but it was typical of the dangerous mining conditions of the age. Immigrant laborers, mainly Irish and German, were paid little, worked under dangerous and squalid conditions, and could look forward to little more than death, injury, or a premature old age. Perhaps not surprisingly, camaraderie was high among the sandhogs. Most of them were first- or second-generation immigrants, and they were bonded to each other by the constant and terrible risks they faced together. Nothing, however, could have steeled them for what was about to happen at Crib #5 on the night of July 24, 1916.

Crib #5 was begun on August 3, 1914. The two existing parallel tunnels connecting the Division Avenue pumping station with Crib #4 would be extended by a single tunnel to a point five miles north of the Cuyahoga River mouth. Crib #5 was towed out and sunk at the five-mile point, and workers from Cribs #4 and #5 began tunneling towards each other. As with previous tunnels, the project was initially put out for bid to private construction companies. Owing, however, to second thoughts about the unhappy history of previous tunnels, the bids were withdrawn and the Cleveland Waterworks Department itself took over the project.

City officials and sandhogs were feeling self-congratulatory about the #5 tunnel as the scorching summer of 1916 passed by. Unlike most previous tunnels, no lives had been lost during two years of work on #5, and the expected link-up with #4 was only a few months away. And Crib #5 and its shaft and tunnel were absolutely state-of-the-art projects. The crib itself was a 100-by-100-foot steel square. In the middle was the shaft, going 128 feet down from the surface of the lake to a point 40 to 50 feet below the lakebed. The shaft contained an elevator for transporting the sandhogs and removing the excavated dirt. At the bottom of the shaft, the new tunnel ran south to a point 1,500 feet from Crib #5 and about 1,200 feet north from the tunnel being pushed toward it from Crib #4. Not far from the crib shaft was a 30-foot airlock with doors on both ends of it, which, together with powerful air compressors at the crib, kept pressure in the tunnel at about 22 pounds per square inch, sometimes more.

The tunnel itself was a pipe, 10 feet in diameter, made out of interlocking concrete blocks, four to a section. A small railway stretched from the bottom of the shaft up to the tunnel face. There, working behind an ingeniously designed hydraulic shield that was progressively forced forward to hold up the ceiling as the miners advanced, a tunneling machine gouged 30-foot arcs out of the sand, gravel, and clay that lay in its path. Workers behind the shelf quickly seized the flying chunks of dirt and threw them into small railroad cars. Taken to the elevator, the cars were hoisted up and emptied over the side of the crib, adding to its sturdy foundation.

Crib #5 was more, however, than just a work site. About 85 men *lived* at the crib, many of them for months at a time. Working in three eight-hour shifts, sandhogs were scheduled for eight hours work, eight hours sleep, and eight hours for whatever recreation one could find on a 100-foot steel platform five miles out in the middle of Lake Erie. During the winter, sandhogs at #5 were virtually marooned, their only link with the shore being infrequent supply boats. There was no radio, no telegraph, and no telephone; a telephone had been tried with previous cribs but the cables were repeatedly severed by ship anchors. All in all, however, Cleveland officials and mine workers took great pride in Crib #5. Technically, it was a sweet achievement and the boast of a department with a bloody history . . . now thought safely put behind it. In reality, Crib #5 was just a terrible accident waiting to happen.

In hindsight, it seems incredible that the disaster was allowed to occur. It was well known to sandhogs and utility officials that natural gas was a danger in both the #4 and #5 tunnels. There had been minor gas explosions in both tunnels during the year previous to July 1916, and workers in #4 complained that the gas made them too sick to work.

The danger became more immediate on Saturday, July 22. That night, William Moore, a shield driver working at the #5 face, saw a sudden, foot-wide rupture in the tunnel floor, and gas rushed out with a roar. Nearly overcome, Moore immediately informed his superiors. That same Saturday, Patrick Delaney, an experienced tunneler, quit his job at #5. He told the boatman who taxied him to shore that "there was enough gas in the tunnel to light the city of Cleveland."

Signs of danger increased on Sunday. Gas forced the midnight shift to quit at 4 a.m., and crew foreman Harry Vokes was ordered to build a bulkhead at the tunnel face. Twenty-four hours later, the Monday morning work crew unanimously refused to even enter the gas-filled tunnel. By then, Gus Van Duzen, the #5 tunnel chief, was aware of the gas problem. On Monday morning he met with Water Commissioner Charles Jaeger and Utilities Director Thomas Farrell and was unequivocally ordered to keep workers out of the tunnel until it tested safe for gas and a broken air compressor was repaired. Van Duzen also had air samples sent to the office of City

Chemist Wilbur S. White for analysis and ordered a ventilator installed at the shaft to help draw gas out of the tunnel.

But at some point Monday evening, July 24, the decision was made to send workers back into the tunnel. How this happened is still not clear: Van Duzen had strict orders not to let workers back into the tunnel until the air had tested safe and the compressor was fixed. Van Duzen also apparently failed to communicate these orders to John Johnston, the Crib #5 superintendent. The tunnel crew chief that evening, Harry Vokes, should have known better, too—but shortly after 8 p.m. he requested permission to take his work crew into the tunnel and John Johnston told him to go ahead, "conditions permitting." In Vokes's work crew were hoisting engineer Thomas Clark; muckers Jack Welsh, John Mackey, and Frank Captain; and miners Stephen Hayes, William Lahnstein, Fred Caplan, and Nickola Samptr. It was a good cross-section of the Cleveland sandhog community. Harry Vokes was a long-time tunnel veteran; he had spent Monday afternoon shopping for baby clothes with his expectant wife, Hazel. Thomas Clark had lived with his wife and nine-year-old daughter for a year in Cleveland; his family eagerly awaited the arrival of paper-hangers in their new home on Tuesday morning. Perhaps the luckiest man in Cleveland that week, however, was J. A. Flynn, a miner who quit on the spot when Johnston asked him to go into the tunnel with his work crew about 8 p.m. Monday.

Only the doomed members of Vokes's work crew, perhaps, heard the fatal gas explosion that occurred at the tunnel face at 9:22 p.m. It was so powerful that it smashed and hurled the heavy concrete tunnel sections around, killing and burying the Vokes crew in a fiery holocaust of flame and dirt.

The first hints that something had gone wrong below came to Engineer H. H. Rinehald at the compressor turbine gauges and to crib elevator operator George Ellis. At 9:22 p.m. they noticed their air gauges fluctuating wildly, shooting up from the normal level of 22 pounds per square inch (psi) to over 30 psi, and then back down to only 5 psi in the tunnel. In addition, Ellis later testified, he could

Gus Van Duzen in the Crib #5 Tunnel.

distinctly smell gas. Crib Superintendent Johnston was immediately notified that something had gone wrong.

Johnston reacted instantly. He tried to telephone Vokes at the tunnel face, but received no answer. Johnston then went down the shaft elevator alone and returned some minutes later to tell the anxious sandhogs topside that the tunnel was filled with gas and that the Vokes crew was trapped somewhere inside. He went down the elevator again, accompanied by a pipe fitter. The two men soon returned, gasping for breath. "Come on boys, we've got to go down for them," shouted Johnston, and he asked for volunteers. Seven men stepped forward, and the rescue party descended the shaft to the airlock below. In the group were Johnston, Peter McKenna, shield driver Archie Turnbull, pipeman Frank Reep, mucker Louis Zappisolli, track finisher Mike Gallagher, William Yeoman, and pipeman James Woods. Armed only with "bugs," as the sandhogs called flashlights, the eight men went through the airlock—and were almost immediately felled by the gas on the other side.

Two Probes in Horror to Begin

EXTRA THE NEWS HOME EDITION

TUNNEL DEATH LIST 21, 10 RESCUERS ARE KILLED

BRINGING IN DEAD; REVIVING TUNNEL VICTIMS

HEROES GIVE UP THEIR LIVES, BUT SAVE ONLY FEW

*Cleveland News* headline.

Peter McKenna saw John Johnston fall to the ground ahead of him. They were only about 100 feet past the airlock, and the staggering McKenna dragged Johnston's unconscious body back toward the airlock. Minutes later, Engineer J. W. Dolan heard a faint tapping coming from the bottom of the crib shaft. He and Foreman H. C. Parson, accompanied by miner Mike Kilbane, descended the shaft. At the bottom they met the heroic McKenna; he, Johnston, and Mike Gallagher would be the only survivors of the initial rescue effort.

The crib platform was now ruled by pandemonium and terror. Communication with Cleveland's safety forces over the next 12 hours would be haphazard at best. But the men at Crib #5 did what they could. By 10 p.m. Rinehald had already sounded the Crib's small steam whistle, sending off the standard distress signal: five short blasts, repeated at intervals. Rockets were fired into the night sky, to explode hundreds of feet above the crib. Owing to smoke and fog on the lakefront, however, the rockets were not seen even by lookouts at the downtown U.S. Lifesaving Station. Nor was the crib's whistle heard. Minutes ticked away, and there was still no sign that anyone on shore had been alerted.

Two residents of Lakewood may have been the first to notice something was wrong. C. G. Prescott of Lake Avenue saw a rocket explode over the lake sometime after 9 p.m. He ran outside, where he could hear the sound of the crib whistle, and he immediately called the U.S. Lifesaving Station. Another alarm was called in by Glen Fuller, also of Lake Avenue. He later testified that he heard the crib whistle about 10 p.m. and later saw some rockets.

As 11 p.m. came, about 90 minutes had elapsed since the explosion, and the men at #5 were frantic. Their greatest need was for pulmotors (mechanical devices used to revive victims of suffocation) and gas masks. Without masks, they couldn't go into the tunnel, and without pulmotors they couldn't revive the rescued sandhogs.

The first response to the Crib #5 distress signals came about 11 p.m., when two boats from the freighter *Star of Jupiter* pulled alongside the crib. The freighter had neither gas masks nor pulmotors, so its only aid was to take McKenna and Johnston to shore for medical treatment.

Minutes after the *Star of Jupiter's* boats departed, about midnight, Captain Hans Hansen of the U.S. Lifesaving Station arrived in a motor launch, greeted by desperate pleas that screaming, frightened men would repeat again and again over the next four hours: "Helmets! Pulmotors! Is there anyone at all who knows anything about air? Oh God! My God! Is there anyone on this boat who knows anything?!"

Shortly after midnight someone contacted Gus Van Duzen at his West-59th-Street home. He immediately departed for Whiskey Island, gathered volunteers, and took a tugboat to #5. Jumping aboard the crib, he shouted, "Who'll volunteer? I'm going down!" Twelve men instantly stepped forward, followed by another five who formed a backup party. Down the shaft went Van Duzen's group and toward the airlock. Almost immediately they were in trouble.

Martin Nelson went down with Van Duzen. The air was tainted with gas and a man next to Nelson stumbled and fell. Nelson felt "funny" but he went forward, spurred by Van Duzen saying, "Keep up, Nelson! Ahead, man, ahead! They're waiting for us out there." Nelson tried to keep going, but he could not. He soon found himself crawling on his hands and knees. Numbness settled over his body. It seemed as though there were a tremendous weight pressing down on his head . . . and the last thing he would remember was trying to lift his face up out of a mud puddle.

Michael Kehoe, another member of the Van Duzen rescue party, also had terrible memories of the experience. He could see the unconscious bodies of the would-be rescuers who had gone ahead. "It was awful to see those men at whose side you had worked in there and yet be unable to save them," he recalled later. "They lay gasping for air on the floor." And the rescue party that followed Van Duzen's band was immediately driven back by gas.

It was now almost 2 a.m. and no effective help had yet arrived at Crib #5. But about an hour after Van Duzen went down the shaft, someone called his wife and told her he was lying dead in the #5 tunnel. "Mrs. Van," as she was affectionately known to the sandhogs, was not one to submit to fate easily. She called her son, Thomas Clancy, at his Public Square taxi stand and told him to go get his stepfather out of the #5 tunnel. Clancy picked up his friend, Thomas Keating, and the two men sped to the waterfront. Commandeering a boat at the West 11th Street Custom House, they arrived at the crib about 3 a.m.—just as the firetug *George A. Wallace* got there, without bringing any gas masks or pulmotors.

Keating and Clancy did not wait for permission from the authorities. Wrapping wet towels around their heads, they descended the shaft. Minutes later they returned, dragging the bodies of Patrick Sullivan, John McCormick, and Harry Hatcher.

It was now almost 4 a.m., seven hours after the tunnel explosion. Precious minutes were slipping away and Water Commissioner Jaeger faced a terrible dilemma. He could have the air pressure taken off in the tunnel, which would make it easier for the

Survivors of the Crib disaster: Mike Gallagher, Lawrence Dunn, and Mike Keough, July 25, 1916.

rescuers to work. But it would also increase the risk of the tunnel walls collapsing. Jaeger had the pressure taken off.

At about 4:45 a.m. the *George A. Wallace* returned, this time with smoke helmets, oxygen tanks, and a pulmotor. Richard Kistenmaker, of the fire department, and Keating donned helmets and together with Clancy, who was completely unprotected, descended the shaft. Minutes later came the expected tapping signal and up came the elevator carrying Kistenmaker, Keating, and the unconscious body of Clancy.

About dawn, more help began to arrive. Most crucial was the arrival of Garrett A. Morgan of the National Safety Device Company of Cleveland. Years earlier, Morgan had invented a gas mask, which he frequently demonstrated to fire departments around the country. John Chafin, a Cleveland policeman, had witnessed one of these demonstrations, and he persuaded Cleveland authorities to get in touch with Morgan in the wee hours of July 25. Within an hour, Morgan arrived at #5 with several of his helmets and accompanied by his brother Frank. The moment had come for the ultimate test of the Morgan gas mask.

Morgan asked for volunteers, but only the ever-heroic Tom Clancy and a man named Thomas Castelbery stepped forward. As the Morgan brothers and the two volunteers prepared to descend, Mayor Harry Davis stepped forward and said, "Goodbye," to Morgan, so doubtful was he of the helmet's effectiveness. The four men disappeared down the shaft.

On his first trip into the tunnel, Garrett Morgan soon stumbled over a body. While the other rescuers removed it, Morgan continued on down the tunnel. Within minutes, he found a man underneath one of the dirt cars, his face in the slime. It was Gus Van Duzen. "It's Dad, and he's alive!" cried Clancy, as they brought the stupefied Van Duzen to the top.

In all, Garrett Morgan made four trips into the tunnel. With help from his companions, he removed, either dead or alive, Van Duzen, Clarence Welch, and other miners, including Yeoman, Schwind, Woods, Turnbull, Reep, Zappisolli, and Banks.

The living and the dead that could be found were removed from the crib by boat, and the injured were taken to hospitals. Now would come the really difficult part: when everyone sat down and decided who was to blame for the deaths of 19 men and the injury of at least 9 others.

First, however, a grisly task had to be performed. Elmer Kisner, the union business agent, went through the clothes of the dead. No one could actually identify what must have been the corpse of George Banks. In his pocket was the newspaper clipping of a poem entitled "Your Little Wife," probably tucked into his wallet by Mrs. Banks that morning. It read:

Who plans to make your future bright?
Your little wife.
Who cooks to tempt your appetite?
Who tells her women friends that you
Are one grand husband thru and thru,

Who's the best girl you ever knew?
Your little wife.

On Archie Turnbull's body was a letter from his mother that read:

> Dear boy. I would like to go and see you. How are you getting on? I hope your cough is better. Don't you need your suit case and clothes? Now Goodbye, and God bless you and keep you safe is the prayer of your mother.

The official city inquest into the disaster opened at 10 a.m. on Thursday, July 27. By this time, the Ohio State Industrial Commission, the U.S. Bureau of Mines, and the U.S. Department of Labor were also promising investigations of the catastrophe. The heat was on Mayor Harry Davis's administration to find someone to blame. Newspaper editorials and the comments of potential witnesses articulated a number of puzzling and explosive questions:

- Why were no physicians on call at #5, as required in the bid specifications demanded of private tunnel contractors offered two years previously?
- Why were there no boats at the crib for communication with the shore—as called for in the private bidding?
- Why were workers allowed to work in the tunnel when the gas level exceeded three percent—a condition prohibited to private contractors?
- Why did a work crew enter the tunnel on Monday evening, contrary to the explicit orders of the Water Commissioner?
- Why were no gas helmets or pulmotors present at Crib #5?
- Why were there no telephone, telegraph, or wireless connections, so that Crib #5 could communicate with the shore?
- Why—perhaps the most important question of all—did at least *seven* hours elapse before effective aid reached the distressed crib?

Despite this intense publicity, the Crib #5 inquest proved anticlimactic. Given the undeniable heroism of many of those involved, the inquest lurched toward an inevitable, indeed predictable verdict. Testimony revealed that the Waterworks Department, city safety officials and the managers of Crib #5 were completely unprepared for the disaster, despite the ample experience of earlier tragedies at other cribs and water tunnels. Gus Van Duzen, John Johnston, and other supervisors admitted that there were no pulmotors or gas masks at #5—and they probably also told the truth when they insisted that there were no such safety frills at comparable mining projects throughout the United States.

The controversy over who was responsible for sending men into the tunnel on Monday night was relatively acrid. Under cross-examination, Van Duzen modified his initial claim that he had explicitly forbidden Harry Vokes to enter the tunnel, finally admitting, after a sensational appearance at the inquest by Vokes's angry widow, Hazel, that he had merely cautioned Vokes that the tunnel wouldn't be in working condition until midnight. Crib Superintendent John Johnston injected a thrill of dramatic tension when he refused to answer two direct questions about what he told Harry Vokes on Monday night. Indeed, on July 23 Assistant County Prosecutor Fred Green told city police to put Johnston under arrest at Lakeside Hospital, where he was recovering from his injuries. But the drama passed quickly. For many reasons those guilty of criminal negligence could not be punished. Both Van Duzen and Johnston were guilty of negligence but they had—thanks to sensationalistic newspaper coverage—become the "heroes" of the disaster. City officials, too, were guilty of gross negligence—but Mayor Harry Davis absolved everyone involved only hours after the inquest had begun with his comment: "I believe every man did what he thought was best. It is easy to criticize, but how does anyone know he wouldn't have done the same under similar circumstances?" The formal inquest verdict held no one responsible for the disaster at all.

Shockingly, Garrett Morgan was not even called as an inquest witness. Worse, his heroism went almost unrecorded in white-owned and staffed Cleveland newspapers. And while James J. Keat-

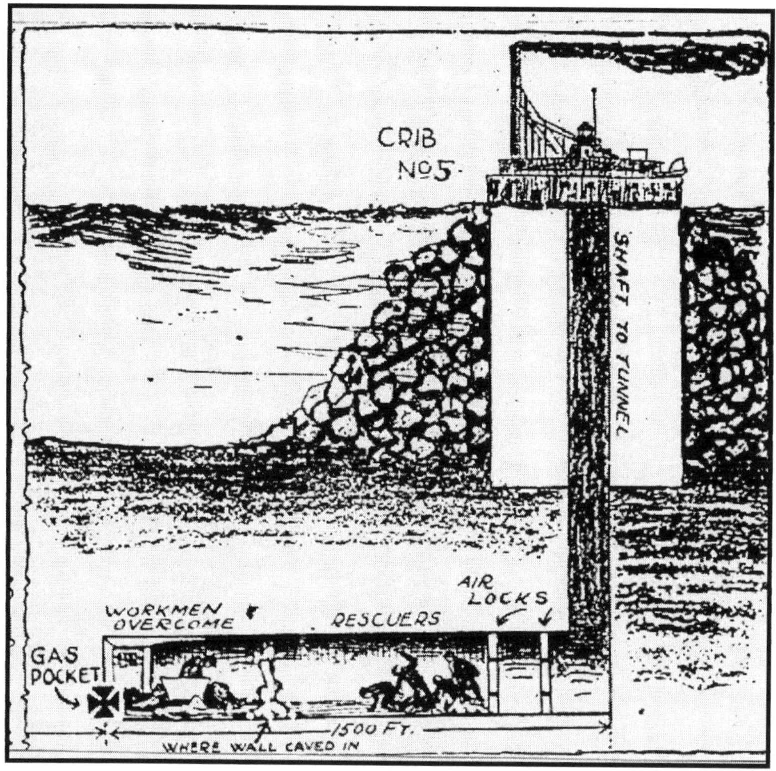


Diagram of Crib #5 and where explosion occurred.

ing, William Dolan, Thomas Clancy, and James McGrath received Carnegie Hero Fund Commission medals for their heroism during the tunnel disaster, the Davis Administration refused to support a medal for Morgan, a slight that embittered Morgan for the rest of his life. Worse still, the city refused to recognize Morgan's claim for compensation for injuries sustained in his rescue work that terrible morning. So much for the hero to whom Mayor Davis had allegedly said on that same morning, "The city will take care of you for the rest of your days."

The Crib #5 inquest petered out in mutterings of recrimination. Meanwhile, work crews had already returned to #5 to dig out the dead. This unspeakable labor went on for almost a month, the discovery of the mutilated, burned, and often dismembered corpses usually preceded by a "disgusting odor" wafting from the ruined tunnel face.

And the legacies of the Crib #5 disaster? The City of Cleveland quickly implemented the safety measures it had previously ignored. The #5 tunnel was eventually finished and became operational in 1918. The State Industrial Commission paid about $3,800 to each of the bereaved families. And Garrett Morgan was eventually recognized as the hero of the Crib #5 tragedy and the genius who invented the automatic traffic light and other useful devices.

A comic footnote to the tragedy was the appearance of Patrick Kearns at Crib #5 on Wednesday, July 26. Thought to be a member of the Vokes crew, Kearns had initially been listed in the tallies of the dead. The truth was somewhat less dramatic. It seems Kearns drew his pay on Monday afternoon and did not show up for work, as scheduled, that evening. He ended up sleeping that night in Edgewater Park, where he was mugged. "I thought you might be glad to know them papers lied," was his insouciant comment on the whole affair.

But perhaps the last word belongs to "Scotty" Jamieson, a miner in the Cleveland Waterworks Department. Jamieson was a relatively unsung hero of the disaster; his name went unmentioned in early press accounts, despite the fact that he helped carry six tunnel victims out himself. His bitter comment to a *Plain Dealer* reporter is the best epitaph for a disaster that never should have happened. When asked what it was like that terrible night, he simply said, "They died crawling in the slime."

# CLEVELAND'S SADDEST FOURTH

## The S. S. Kresge Fireworks Explosion (1908)

You wouldn't know to look at it now. If you drive by 2025 Ontario Street today you might easily miss it. The location is now just an anonymous-looking business office. But on July 3, 1908, that address became history—terrible history, indeed—although it is almost completely forgotten today. You'd never guess, to look at its modern glass-and-trim front, that it was once the scene of a fiery, exploding holocaust that brought death to seven, injury to dozens, and a day of terror, tears, heroism, and shame to the city of Cleveland. For this is the site of the S. S. Kresge fireworks explosion and fire.

Let us set the stage for the chief actors in this melancholy tale. For Anna and Freda Trefall, sisters and fellow clerks at the Ontario S. S. Kresge store, the fateful day began early. They got up at 6 a.m. at their 2308 Carnegie Avenue boarding house, lest they be tardy when the dime store opened at 9 a.m. sharp. Anna and Freda were orphans from Wisconsin, who had come to Cleveland a year previously to live with their sister-in-law. Everyone noticed how close they were to each other; the coming day would offer sublime proof of their sisterly bond.

Mary Hughes, 27, of Whitman Avenue didn't work at the Kresge store. She was an assistant to a downtown dressmaker. But the necessities of her job would bring her to the Ontario dime store that morning to buy some material for her work.

Ed Bolton didn't work for the S. S. Kresge Company either. But his day as a shipping clerk at the W. P. Southworth store next door began early, too, and he expected to spend it slaving over the mountain of orders that had to go out before the July 4th holiday. Ed came from a surprisingly heroic bloodline: his uncle, Captain John Grady, had bravely lost his life fighting a terrible 1891 Cleveland fire, and three other uncles were members of the Cleveland Fire Department.

The day came early, too, for Jimmy Parker, four years old, of Hampden Avenue. Jimmy's father, George Parker, had promised Jimmy that this year he could join in the noisy fireworks at the Parker home. But first, Jimmy Parker had to go shopping downtown with his mother, Minnie . . .

Up early also that fine July morning was Luther Roberts, the janitor of the Kresge store. Luther was short, quiet and self-effacing—but his incredible courage would resound throughout the city before the day was done.

Winifred Duncan was excited that morning. Only 18, one of the many teenaged clerks at Kresge's, she usually sold postcards on the first floor. But today she was going to do something unusual . . . and thereby step unwittingly into history.

The S. S. Kresge store occupied the first two floors of a four-story structure, with a restaurant in the basement and offices on the third and fourth floors. Toward the center and rear of the ground floor, a stairway rose upward, dividing at a landing into left and right flights to the second floor. From the right side of the landing, a balcony stretched out over the right rear of the store, forming a mezzanine level that contained the manager's office. The second floor was generally unobstructed, with windows both at the front on Ontario Street and the back, facing an alley, where there was also a fire escape. The only dangerously obscure aspect of the building was this: although there was a rear exit to the building on the left side of the first-floor staircase, there was no exit whatsoever

S. S. Kresge store with fire department ladders raised, July 3, 1908.

in the identical-looking area to the right of the staircase. There, instead of an exit, were three windows, blocked with temporary shelves and further secured with steel bars, wire netting, and sheet-iron doors to prevent break-ins from the rear alley. Under normal circumstances this layout presented no problem. But if someone were in a hurry to get out the back of the store and turned to the right of the staircase instead of the left . . . it might make all the difference between life and death.

Owing to the ensuing deaths and the confusion of the tragedy, we cannot know the exact sequence of events that day. We do know, however, that at about 10:50 that Friday morning, Mrs. Minnie Parker and her four-year-old son Jimmy entered the Kresge store.

Jimmy had been lured there by the sight of clerk Winifred Duncan, demonstrating a sizzling sparkler near the store's front window. D. E. Greene, the store manager, had just ordered her to do so and had assured her that the sparklers were "harmless." Winifred stood in the aisle, three feet wide, separating the postcard department from the ample counters of firecrackers, Roman candles, rockets, and sparklers that were stacked all over the first floor in that era of virtually unregulated Fourth of July mayhem.

This was the scene in Kresge's as 10:50 a.m. arrived: Minnie and Jimmy Parker were watching Winifred demonstrate a sparkler. Manager Greene was in his mezzanine office with Cashier Celia Zak, scanning the day's mail. Mrs. Fannie Frank, 50, a Collinwood Village matron, was shopping on the second floor with her four-year-old granddaughter, Grace. Mary Hughes, the dressmaker's assistant, was probably in the sewing section on the second floor. Ed Bolton was next door at the Southworth Company, busily getting out the day's orders. Miss Carrie Bubel, a clerk, was selling goods at her counter on the second floor. Erma Schumacher, 18, was pacing the floor, keeping a vigilant eye on the 50 or so female clerks who worked the floor. Although only 18, Erma had just been promoted to floorwalker, and it was well known that she aspired to even higher rank. Muriel Mayes, a Kresge clerk, was at her second floor counter. So, too, was Freda Trefall, while her older sister Anna worked downstairs. Mary Podowski, a charwoman, was awaiting change from the $20 bill she had handed a clerk. Andrew Lempke, a Kresge employee, was trimming lamps as he worked atop a ladder on the first floor. And staff pianist Hazel Thompson, one of the several Kresge pianists who demonstrated the store's sheet music for curious customers, had just launched into a rendition of "I Don't Want to Go Home in the Dark" . . . when all hell broke loose on the first floor.

This is probably what happened. After remarking to Minnie and Jimmy Parker that her sparkler was "perfectly harmless," Winifred turned sideways toward a fireworks display that included an American flag. Sparks from the sparkler in her hand suddenly ignited the fabric of the flag, which in turn set fire to Mrs. Parker's voluminous, flammable dress. As the two terrified women attempted to beat out the flames, sparks from the dress fell on adjacent fireworks coun-

Water Tower in action at a subsequent fire, Oct. 29, 1909.

ters and the fire and explosions began their deadly race through the store.

It was about as close to instantaneous combustion as you can get. The store contained about $30,000 worth of fireworks, and within seconds of the initial spark, the entire stock ignited in an inferno of blazing colors, dense smoke, and terrifying, deafening explosions. In a minute or less the entire first floor of Kresge's was a fiery nightmare, with up to 200 panic-stricken shoppers and clerks trying to flee the sudden conflagration. Max Zucker, a customer on the ground floor, had a typical experience. One moment he was staring at the sizzling electric sparkler, and the next: "I heard a sputtering noise—a skyrocket whizzed past my face and darted over the heads of the crowd and set fire to combustible material on the counters. People around me stood aghast for a few seconds. A giant cracker exploded with a roar that set all into a mad dash for the front and rear exits."

The fire spread with shocking speed, setting merchandise and people alike on fire as it raced from counter to counter, aisle to aisle

YOUR VACATION

The Cleveland Press.

LAST EDITION

# SIX PERSONS ARE DEAD IN FIRE AT AN ONTARIO STREET STORE

Scores of Women Hurt by Leaping From Burning Kresge Building.

BODIES OF BOY AND FIVE WOMEN ARE FOUND IN REAR OF BURNED STORE AFTER BLAZE IS OUT

Mad Panic of Clerks and Customers When Fireworks Start Flames—Dead Evidently Tried in Vain to Open Door to Escape

SCENES AT FIRE WHERE SIX PERISHED

DEAD AND INJURED

THE DEAD.

The bodies of five women and one boy were found in the rear of the building.

INJURED.

*Cleveland Press* headline.

through the store. The next morning's *Plain Dealer* well conveyed the horror of the next few minutes:

> Big piles of fireworks exploded and added to the noise and confusion. Giant crackers pounded and boomed, skyrockets whizzed through the crowded room, roman candles sputtered and flashed. It was a mimic battle, magnificent if it had not been so full of terror and death.

Several patterns of movement developed during the fire's first minutes. On the blazing first floor, customers tried to escape in three directions. Those near the front headed for the Ontario exit. For those toward the rear, the aisles to the left and right of the rear center staircase beckoned toward seeming safety. This was true of the aisle to the left, a corridor that led to an unlocked door on the back alley. The corridor to the right of the staircase, however, led only to the rear wall of the store, blocked there by shelving and barred windows.

Things were better on the second floor. When it became apparent there that the first floor was afire, movement surged toward the front and rear windows, the elevator, and the staircase. The elevator was not working, and it was immediately abandoned after one attempt to use it. Most of the shoppers and clerks fled to the front and back windows and most of them survived, albeit injured and traumatized. Some, however, tried to escape down the stairs, and the vast crush and hysterical panic there quickly precipitated a pile-up of screaming, suffocating women, girls and children on the stairs and the landing on the ground floor. All of them were pulled out or managed to wriggle free and stagger into the inferno waiting below.

The evidence is that the fire department arrived soon after the fire started, but by the time the engines got there, Kresge's was already a fiery pyre, with smoke pouring out of every door and window. Customers and employees were still streaming out of the exits and frightened women were leaping out the second floor windows. Firemen quickly deployed ladders and nets. The nets saved many lives but could not prevent some terrible injuries. Owing to the smoke, many could not even see the nets and fell beyond them to the pavement below. And quite a number of people jumped into the same nets simultaneously, injuring each other and bringing the nets crashing to the ground.

Let us see how our cast of characters fared. Poor little Jimmy Parker disappeared into the interior of the store during the first few panicky moments of the fire. His mother, although badly burned, frantically searched the burning store for Jimmy. Told, however, that a little boy had been rescued from the store, she was persuaded to leave and return home. By the time she got there her husband George had already identified Jimmy's corpse at the county morgue.

D. E. Greene, the Kresge store manager, did his best. As he was in the middle of sorting his mail, an exploding firecracker alerted him to the danger. He immediately seized cashier Celia Zak and rushed her to safety outside on Ontario Street. He then returned and tried to save others until flames and smoke drove him back out into the street for good.

The chief hero of the Kresge tragedy was Luther Roberts, the Kresge janitor. Realizing that the elevator was useless, he began to smash open the windows on the second floor. He then went to the fatal staircase, clogged with screaming, writhing, piled-up bodies and began to drag and throw them out the back windows of the second floor onto the fire escape. Time after time, Roberts returned to the staircase, until the flames and smoke drove him back, "blinded and dizzy." But he had cleared everybody from the staircase.

Roberts's courage, if not his fate, was matched by that of Anna Trefall. When the fire started, 24-year-old Anna was working with several clerks on the first floor. Her companions immediately seized her and tried to drag her out the Ontario exit. She resisted, saying, "I must find my sister!" She broke free and ran toward the staircase to get to Freda on the second floor. Her first attempt failed; the hysterical sea of bodies surging down the staircase soon forced her back toward the Ontario exit and safety. But she again freed herself from the crowd and resumed the search for her 17-year-old sister. We don't know the exact sequence of events after that, except that Freda was one of the last to make it down the staircase during the fire. Upon reaching the ground floor, she was immediately overwhelmed in the pile-up of terrified women there. An eyewitness saw Anna try to pull Freda toward the Ontario exit, and then saw both sisters stumble and fall to the floor. Freda and Anna Trefall died with the rest of those trapped by the three barred windows, their arms around each other's necks. Freda's dead face was so crazed with fear that her fellow employees could not identify her corpse.

Ed Bolton, too, proved himself a hero that July day. Becoming aware of the fire, he ran into the burning building. He dragged several persons out of the building onto Ontario and then reentered the store on his hands and knees to search for others, until the fire drove him out again. He then held nets for those leaping from the second floor.

This almost proved Bolton's undoing. As a girl prepared to leap

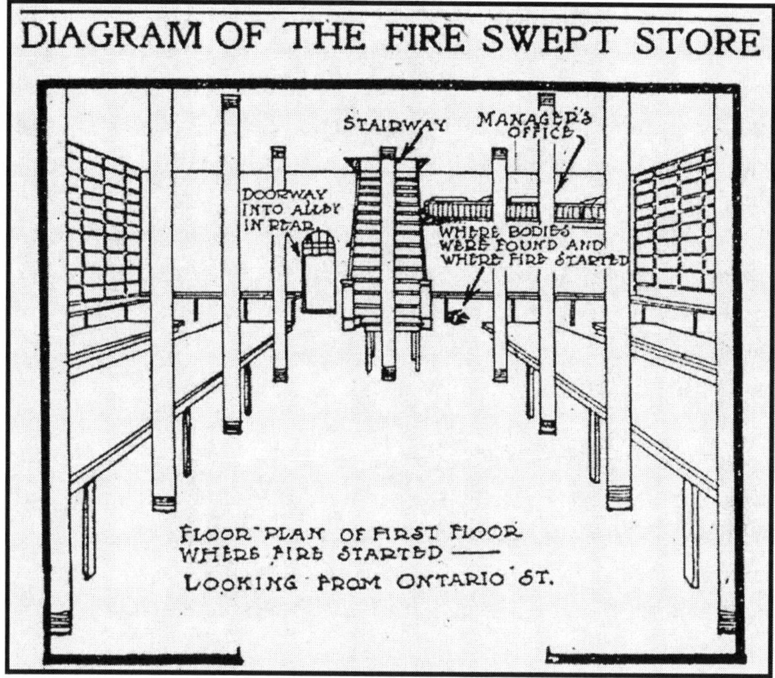


Simplified diagram of the S. S. Kresge 1st Floor (from the *Plain Dealer.*)

from the second floor, she opened her umbrella like a parachute to aid in breaking her fall. By the time Bolton shouted, "Never mind your umbrella," it was already too late. As the young lady landed in the net, her umbrella smashed Bolton's arm, breaking it and sending him out of the fray. Staying in character, Bolton merely had his broken arm set, returned home to change out of his wet clothing, and resumed shipping out the holiday orders for Southworth Company, Grocers Wholesale and Retail.

Mary Hughes was just in the wrong place at the wrong time. The dressmaker's assistant survived the crushing pile-up at the staircase—only to die with the rest of the victims by the three back barred windows.

Mrs. Fannie Frank of Collinwood was a heroine, too, that July day. On the second floor with her four-year-old granddaughter,

Grace, Mrs. Frank quickly led the child to a window and out onto a projecting ledge. From there she jumped, holding Grace so as to shield her from the impact of the fall. Fannie hit the ground, injuring herself but saving Grace from injury. As Fannie put it, "I could not bear to think of what my daughter would say if the child was hurt."

Erma Schumacher, the newly promoted floorwalker, died in character. When the fire started, she tried to stem the panic of her employees at the flashpoint—the staircase—and it was near there and by the three barred back windows that firemen found her body later in the afternoon.

Muriel Mayes, a second-floor clerk, was one of the first to escape from the second floor. At first she thought the explosions were the work of mischievous boys blowing off fireworks in the rear alley, but she eventually made her way to a front window and was the first person to jump into the nets below. She survived the jump, but was badly injured by the force of collision with the bodies that jumped into the net after her.

Miss Emma Schaef, 17, was something of a heroine, too, after a fashion. She had fled to the second-floor windows looking out on Ontario. There was a woman with a child there, afraid to jump through the suffocating smoke toward the nets below. So Emma pushed them out toward the net below. The woman missed it, hitting the sidewalk. Then Emma jumped—and missed it, too. The child was unhurt.

Miss Carrie Bubel, 18, had one of the fire's typical injuries. Selling goods on the second floor when the fire started, she was paralyzed by terror for some minutes. By the time she got to the windows, everyone else had already jumped. She jumped, missing the net, breaking her left leg and spraining her right.

Let us not forget charwoman Mary Podowski. Just as she handed her $20 bill to a clerk, the fire exploded around her. Initially disoriented by the blaze, Mary recovered her nerve and began searching through the burning, smoky store for the clerk who had taken her money. After fighting her way into the store through the fright-

STAYS TO SAVE SISTER AND BOTH DIE

**Anna Trefall.**

Heroine and martyr was Anna Trefall at the Kresge store fire yesterday. She died while trying to save her little sister Freda. The two were found by the firemen with arms locked around each other's neck.

The two girls were working in dif-

Anna and Freda Trefall.

ened crowd surging out, Mary finally spotted the clerk who had taken her $20 bill: "I want my money! Give it to me!" she shrieked. The clerk, who must have marvelled at Mary's single-mindedness, muttered, "Haven't got it!," as the surging, terrified mob swept the clerk by Mary and toward the Ontario exit. After the fire was extinguished, Mary could be seen, still in front of the smoldering store, weeping and sobbing over and over again, "My money! I want my twenty-dollar bill!"

The fire was over in about an hour. It had quickly gutted both floors of the dime store and outside the smoldering ruin milled multitudes of firemen, policemen, and spectators—the latter doing their usual best to impede the work of safety forces. The initial belief was that everyone had been rescued from the burning building. It wasn't until about 12:30 p.m. that Fire Chief George A. Wallace and a crew of searchers entered the sizzling building and found seven bodies in the rear right alcove by the three barred windows. Captain James Granger of Cleveland Fire Company #1 (later chief of the Cleveland Fire Department) described the gruesome scene to a reporter from the *Cleveland Leader*:

> "I heard what sounded like the mewing of a cat," he said. "I had heard that sound before, however, and I shuddered. . . . [There] was a mass of humanity, it seemed, intertwined. There were [six] women. It seemed all had huddled together in the belief they would get air at that particular point, and when the fumes of the powder and paper became too strong all had given up at the same time. The arms of [most] of them were free, but their legs were intertwined so that it would have been impossible for any one to have dragged herself out. At the farther end of the bunch was a little lad. He was living."

The lad was Jimmy Parker, who died soon after his removal from the store. The fact that he was still living when found may have led to the false report that convinced his mother he had survived.

By now, it had begun to rain, and the bodies were removed and laid in the muddy back alley behind the Kresge store. It soon became apparent, however, that two of the victims were still breathing. Two female trained nurses forced themselves through the police line and tried to revive the two survivors. Their efforts were in vain: Erma Schumacher was dead on arrival at Lakeside Hospital later that afternoon. The other survivor, S. S. Kresge clerk Elizabeth Reis, recovered consciousness at Huron Road Hospital before dying at 6:30 that evening.

The awful afternoon was not yet finished. While police and firemen searched the smoking ruins of the store and questioned survivors, heartbreaking scenes unfolded at the county morgue, where most of the seven bodies had been taken. Through it streamed a mournful procession of relatives, survivors, and a goodly proportion of the morbidly curious to see and identify the dead. Catching sight of his dead four-year-old son, George Parker collapsed, sobbing, "My son, my son! My poor little Jimmy!" Two sisters of Mary Hughes identified her corpse—by her teeth—but then became hysterical and had to be led away. Throughout that ghastly July afternoon crawled a sad procession of stunned men and women through that house of death, all with the same, simple, sad question on their lips, "Is my girl here?"

The rest of the S. S. Kresge fire saga—except for the ultimate legal result—is the stuff of sour anti-climax. The inquest, managed by Coroner Burke, began on July 9 and featured a parade of witnesses, rigorous cross-examination, and a lot of contradictory testimony. Winifred Duncan testified about her sparkler demonstration—but firmly denied that it caused the blaze. All witnesses corroborated her belief and that of the store management that the sparklers were "harmless." Testimony disclosed that no one in the store knew that the right rear windows were barred—or even that there were windows there at all. Testimony also revealed that there had never been a fire drill in the Kresge store—and that it was not legally required. As to the display and storage of fireworks, all officials and witnesses agreed that it was in full compliance with all Cleveland fire and safety laws. Or as Coroner Burke lamely summarized the inquest: "I am satisfied that the law was violated in spirit, while it seemed no one was legally culpable. It was morally wrong for that condition to be permitted to exist." The inquest concluded with the finding that while the fire was due to "carelessness in handling fireworks," no one was legally at fault because everyone involved acted under the belief that the sparkler was "harmless."

That wasn't quite the end of the matter. Cleveland newspapers cultivated public outrage over the fire for several weeks afterwards. And the enduring outcome of the Kresge tragedy was a public demand for an end to the homicidal mayhem that had become the norm for Fourth of July celebrations. On July 6, 1908, Cleveland Councilman Daniel Pfahl introduced the following ordinance in Council:

> That no person, firm or corporation, shall, within the city, sell, offer for sale or have in his or its possession or custody any toy pistol, squib, rocket crackers or roman candles or other combustible fireworks, or any article for making of a pyrotechnic display.

The Pfahl ordinance passed Cleveland Council by a vote of 21 to 11 on the night of Monday, July 13, 1908, and was soon signed into law by Mayor Tom Johnson. This landmark legislation and the tragedy that precipitated it were important milestones in the movement, ultimately nationwide, to end the annual toll of deaths and injuries due to fireworks. Other cities and states copied the Cleveland fireworks law and the Pfahl ordinance is remembered now as a pioneer triumph in the crusade for a "safe and sane" Fourth of July. So the Kresge Seven did not die entirely in vain—something to think about the next time you are stalled in traffic opposite 2025 Ontario Street.

# "HORROR OF ALL HORRORS!"

## The Central Viaduct Disaster (1895)

There are several good places to begin the story of the 1895 Central Viaduct tragedy. One of them is down in Cleveland's "Flats." A walk or drive through its maze of crowded, truncated streets offers a quick appreciation of the transportation challenges Clevelanders faced before the construction of high-level bridges in the early 20th century. Cross-town traffic was perpetually stymied by congestion in the Flats' crowded streets and the constant interruptions caused by drawbridges being raised to let river traffic pass. If only a high-level bridge could be built . . .

Another place to begin the Viaduct story is down by the Cuyahoga River itself. Although cleaner now than in 1895, the river at the disaster site is still crooked, muddy, and relatively shallow. It does not look like a friendly place to fall, and one's eyes instinctively gauge the yawning distance from the massive Innerbelt Bridge above to the river below. Perhaps the best place to begin the Viaduct tragedy, however, is in the air, or more exactly, on the tracks of the RTA Rapid Transit bridge situated but a few feet from where the Central Viaduct once thrust across the Cuyahoga a century ago. Sometime on a dark and stormy night, say in November, you might want to take a Rapid and watch, carefully, as it rolls across the steel truss span over the Cuyahoga River below. Look down, then, and think: *Yes, that would be a long way to fall . . . and what if I hit something hard on the way down?*

Like most of Cleveland's civic improvements, the Central Viaduct did not come easily. Agitation for a bridge to Cleveland's expanding South Side preceded completion of the Superior Viaduct and was intensified by South Side resentment of the civic and commercial advantages enjoyed by its neighbors to the north. South Side Councilman James M. Curtiss first introduced a Council resolution in March 1879, asking that the city engineer investigate the best location for a south viaduct. This being Cleveland, however, years of bickering went by before construction finally began on April 26, 1886.

As developed by City Engineer C. G. Force, and later by Walter W. Rice, the Central Viaduct was actually a series of two complementary bridges. The first, the "Central Viaduct" proper, was a 2,839-foot series of spans that stretched from Central Avenue (today a point just south of the juncture of Ontario Avenue and the Hope Memorial Bridge) in a straight line southwest across the Cuyahoga valley to Jennings Avenue (today West 14th Street). The second bridge, a stretch of 1,088 feet, ran over Walworth Run and connected Abbey Avenue with Lorain Avenue—a section still in use today. The Central Viaduct proper was a "stilt" bridge: a series of 20 steel pan-shaped spans supported on stone piers; the length of the spans varied from 30 feet to 236½ feet. Elevation above the Flats was 89 feet over land, 101 feet over the Cuyahoga River.

A problematic feature of the bridge was its pivoting center span which crossed the Cuyahoga River. Built on a pier which jutted up from the center of the river, the center span rested on a turntable which allowed turning to permit river traffic to pass by. Completing the bridge furnishings were 2,000-candle-power electric arc lights, spaced 270 feet apart on 32-foot-high poles. From the very beginning, it was assumed that electric street car tracks would occupy the main 40-foot-wide roadway.

In later years it would be claimed that the Central Viaduct was

SUNDAY SPECIAL 1 P.M. **The Cleveland Press.** GREAT ACCIDENT

# HORROR OF ALL HORRORS!!

## Nothing Like It Has Been Recorded in the History of the Forest City.

### A Motor Car, Loaded With People, Plunges From the Dizzy Heights of the Central Viaduct.

Eighteen Corpses Are Being Mourned Over by Bereaved Friends, and the Motorman Has Been Taken in Hand by the Police Authorities.

Crushed to Death or Smothered in the Mud at the Bottom of the Cuyahoga River---Scenes of Excitement in Which Thousands of People Took Part---Identification of All the Dead Not Yet Arrived At---The List of Those Who Have Been Identified---Interviews With the Motorman the Passengers Who Escaped and People Who Saw the Accident.

*Cleveland Press* headline.

an "unlucky" bridge from the start. It is undeniable that its fearful reputation began with a bang on the afternoon of January 5, 1888. Two men, Harry Burton and Daniel Ockel, were crushed to death when a heavy derrick at the edge of the bridge fell on them. the *Cleveland Press* did not stint on the gory details:

> Ockel's head was severed from his body above the lower jaw. His heart and lungs were lacerated and torn out near the left shoulder which, with the left arm, was mangled and hung by shreds of flesh to the neck. The whole upper part of the body was crushed in. The right leg was fractured above and below the knee, and the left leg was fractured at the ankle.

Not to be outdone, the *Plain Dealer* reported:

> A double handful of brains stained an iron support which had crushed the skull of a victim, and a pool of human blood lying underneath the confused mass marked the place where another had fallen.

The dead were buried in Erie Cemetery and construction continued.

December 11, 1888, was the happy, if cold day on which the Central Viaduct was opened and dedicated. It began with a parade at 2 p.m. and climaxed with a palatial banquet at the Hollenden Hotel. That evening's paroxysm of civic boosterism, with its unmistakable tone of Cleveland-on-the-make was, perhaps, best captured by William R. Rose, then a journalist for the *Cleveland Sun and Voice,* in some doggerel composed for the occasion, which concluded with fulsome praise for James Curtiss, the tireless champion for the South Side bridge:

In coming generations when
Our children's children tell
The famous stories of the past—
The tales they love so well—
With cheering and with laughter
One deed they'll keep alive,
How well brave Curtius saved his bridge
In eighteen eighty-five!

But not everyone was happy with the Viaduct, as this satirical *Press* reply to Rose's paean demonstrated:

I stood on the bridge at midnight
And nobody stood with me,
As the moon rose over the City
With a tax rate of 2.83.

I saw the moon's reflection
In the river flowing free,
And it looked like the plat of some real estate
In a city taxed 2.83.

The Central Viaduct opened just at the time Cleveland's street railways were undergoing full conversion from horse-drawn to electrically-driven cars, and soon the bridge was carrying thousands of Clevelanders per day on the Cleveland Electric Railway's ("Big Consolidated" or "Big Con") Cedar-Jennings line. And the bridge seemed, immediately, to fulfill the expectations of its proponents. But three years after its opening, sometime in late 1892, another "unlucky" incident occurred. Two crowded, speeding streetcars were crossing the Viaduct when one of them jumped the tracks and crashed point-blank into the other. The cars were totalled and there were a large number of dead and wounded.

As with the Superior Viaduct, the main drawback of the Central Viaduct was the bottleneck at its pivoting center draw. Owing to river traffic, it had to be opened and closed several hundred times a month. Jammed streetcars, pedestrian traffic, and horse-drawn vehicles simply had to wait, fuming and fretting, for three to six minutes while the draw was opened and closed. It was frustrating to both river and bridge users—and as Clevelanders would discover, extremely dangerous.

In theory, the Central Viaduct tragedy should never have happened. There were a number of safeguards designed to prevent bridge traffic from entering the open draw. There were a pair of four-foot gates located about 14 feet from both the western and eastern ends of the draw. In addition, there were—or were supposed to be—red warning lights on the gates. When the draw was opened, the bridge tender would hoist an additional red warning light on a pole 10 feet high over the gates.

Additional safeguards had been installed on the viaduct by 1895. About 200 feet from the eastern end of the draw and about 170 feet from the western end were derailleur switches. In order for a streetcar to proceed any further, the conductor or motorman had to stop the car, disembark, and manually pull the derailleur switch. Should they fail to do so, the streetcar would automatically be diverted to a dead-end stop at the side of the viaduct, well short of the gates and the draw. There was also an electrical "cut-off" switch located more than 500 feet from the draw that automatically shut off all electrical power to streetcars when the draw was open. But sometime during the first week of November 1895 the cut-off on the eastern side of the draw shorted out. It is not known to this day whether the employees who daily drove the cars of the Cedar-Jennings "Big Con" line were ever told that the cut-off was out of order.

Dusk comes early to Cleveland in mid-November. It was already dark as many weary travellers trudged or drove to and across the spans of the Central Viaduct around 7 p.m. on November 16, 1895. It was Saturday, always a busy shopping day for Clevelanders, and an opportunity to visit relatives in other parts of the city. Thousands were out on the streets, on horses, and in streetcars despite the dark and a mild drizzle that fell throughout the evening. Let us mingle with them as the chill fall mist falls on what will, for 17 of them, be the last evening of their lives.

Edward Hoffman is the car conductor on Car #642 of the Cedar-Jennings line this evening. Born in Germany and only 23 years old, he has worked for "Big Con" for two years, mostly at the car barns, and before that at John D. Rockefeller's Forest Hills estate. Popular with passengers, Edward has a wife and small child waiting up for his arrival home at the end of the evening. Running from the East End (near Lake View Cemetery), Car #642 leaves Blue Rock Spring (a popular mineral springs resort then located near where the RTA tracks now cross Cedar Avenue in University Circle) about 6:50 p.m. and arrives, via Cedar most of the way, at Public Square at 7:22 p.m. Several passengers get off there and several more get on; more will disembark and embark when the car reaches the Central-Ontario stop just before the viaduct. Fifty-two fares in all will be collected by Conductor Hoffman on that #642 run; only about half of the passengers will be on the car as it lurches onto the Central Viaduct at about 7:30 p.m.

Edward Dahlke is the commander of the tugboat "Ben Campbell" on the Cuyahoga River that night. As 7:30 p.m. comes, his boat is towing the *Abram Smith*, a loaded lumber barge, upstream. As the tug approaches the bridge, Dahlke blows his tug's whistle to alert the bridge tender to open the draw and let him pass.

Captain Charles Brenner is the officer in charge of the draw this night. From his booth on the north side of the Viaduct, located near

Sketch of car #642 falling through the draw.

the safety gates, he hears the tug's whistle and rings five bells to signal the bridge engineer in the draw pier to open the draw. He then (or so he and Agust Inon, his opposite number on the south side of the viaduct, will later testify) raises a red lantern on a pole 10 feet high to alert the tug that the viaduct is about to open. Brenner and Inon then close the safety gates. Car #642 pulls up to the derailleur switch.

Augustus Rogers is the motorman at the controls of Car #642

that drizzly evening. As he brings the car to a stop at the derailleur, Conductor Hoffman jumps down, pulls the derailleur switch and then signals Rogers to proceed. He moves the car controls and #642 began to accelerate toward the draw.

John Stringer is one of four or five men standing on the rear platform of #642 as it moves toward the draw. Like his companions, he is standing outside the car door because he wants to smoke. As the car begins to move, he throws away his cigar stub and prepares to reenter the car. At that moment, someone asks him for a light, momentarily distracting him . . . and inadvertently saving his life. The cast is in place; the tragedy occurs.

Captain Brenner saw the whole thing happen. As car left the derailleur, picking up speed, he ran out of his booth, screaming, "Stop! Stop!" at Rogers the motorman. Within seconds, the car reached the gates, and, as Brenner and another bystander tried to hold the gates, it smashed through and rumbled straight towards the open draw only 14 feet away.

Motorman Rogers may have been the first on the car to realize the mortal peril approaching. As #642 approached the gates, he suddenly noticed that they were closed, and screamed "Jump!"—suiting the action to the word and landing in a bruised heap at the edge of the open draw.

John Serringer was another smoker on the rear platform of the doomed car. He had boarded #642 at Public Square and was paying little attention as he watched Hoffman throw the derailleur switch and felt the car start up again. The next thing he remembered was someone shouting, "Jesus, Stop! Stop! For the love of God, Stop!" Serringer lunged for the safety gates as Car #642 tipped over the edge of the draw . . . and the sudden upward lurch of the trolley's rear as it pitched over threw him to the safety of the Viaduct deck.

Passenger John Mendik, a professor of athletics at the Sokol Nova School, had an even closer call. Seated in the third seat from the rear of the car, he heard the cry of "Jump!" and saw men on the rear platform leaping for the bridge deck. He would long remember the faces in #642 as Death announced its arrival in the car:

> The grewsome picture of startled, death-staring faces, and what transpired in that one dread moment, would take up hours of painful description, and baffle my attempt. All were on their feet, save the mother and child, and whether it was cool self-possession, unconcerned despair or resignation to God's will that prompted such remarkable composure in the face of such danger, I am at a loss to know.

Mendik somehow got through the rear door, onto the platform, and was hurled five feet into the air by the sudden tilt of the car's plunge over the side. He landed on the deck, badly bruised, severely gashed on the head, but alive. Charles Clark, Andrew Radke, G. O. Ross, and Jacob Heller also leapt to safety from the rear of the trolley. Seconds later, they heard a terrifying crash, far below.

James Patterson, the viaduct engineer inside the draw pier, did not actually see the accident, but that was only because he covered his face in horror as he watched the car careen over the edge. But many witnesses had a clear view as the car, travelling between four and six miles per hour, crashed through the safety gates and went over the precipice. It must have been terrible to watch. The car, impelled by its forward motion, did not fall at once, but continued its horizontal progress for a few seconds. Then, as its interior lights went out (when it lost contact with its overhead wire), and as its passengers screamed in terror, it plunged 101 feet, almost hitting the tugboat "Ben Campbell," and smashing into the foundation of the draw pier, sending a 100-foot column of water into the air. Then came a sizzling sound as the broken car settled at a 60-degree angle in the muddy water. And then . . . silence.

Rescue efforts began immediately. Oddly enough, the first alarm was turned in by Harry Rebbeck, a Cleveland fireman, who had also turned in the first alarm on the January 5, 1888, viaduct construction tragedy. Within minutes Captain Dahlke, Motorman Rogers, and other witnesses had gotten in touch with Cleveland's safety forces and aid converged on the accident scene by land and water.

The scene they discovered there was a ghastly one. Clothing

was floating in the river, including four ladies' hats, three men's hats, a large fur cape, a black lisle thread glove, three aprons, an olive-green waist, and a coffee-colored canteen. The smashed-up car was sticking up several feet out of the river, and groaning and gurgling sounds were coming from the frightful wreckage. The groaning came from Patrick Looney. Seated in Car #642, he had noticed the agitation of the other passengers, and managed to make it to the rear platform as the car went over the edge. Incredibly, he survived the ride down, clinging to the car railing, and he remembered the collision with the draw pier. That impact, fracturing his skull, knocked him out for a few seconds. When he came to, he was under water and he was conscious of a humming in his ears. He came to the surface and began to moan. As rescuers tenderly transferred him from the wreck to a makeshift raft, he screamed, "My God, won't you take me from this death? Don't let me die here! Help me to safety!"

The gurgling sound didn't last long. It came from Mrs. Eliza Sauernheimer. Trapped in the wreckage with a crushed right arm and skull, and internal injuries, Eliza lived only five more minutes, as rescuers J. F. Brown and John Welch of the tugboat "Spranckel" held her bleeding head above water while others frantically worked to free her body from the debris. Everyone else in the car—16 people—had already drowned or been smashed to pieces. Several physicians, including Dr. A. B. Schneider of nearby Jennings Avenue, made their way to the river that terrible night to offer aid, but there was nothing for them to do but watch as rescue attempts quickly turned into retrieval of the dead from the ruined streetcar.

That unspeakable task went on for almost two days and was hampered by a number of factors. Chief among them was the condition of the car; it had broken up badly on impact and many of the bodies were trapped under the wreckage. Several early attempts to raise the car succeeded only in breaking it into more pieces. The muddy bottom of the Cuyahoga River was an additional impediment: city diver Walter Metcalf spent many hours wandering

Spectators crowd Central Viaduct to gawk at the search for bodies, Nov. 17, 1895.

amid its mucky depths, while city police and firemen grappled with hooks, mostly in vain, for corpses.

Matters were not helped by the behavior of the populace. Within minutes of the accident, thousands of curious Clevelanders converged on the scene, some of them pickpockets who plied a lucrative trade amid the milling rubberneckers. All streetcar lines to the area became jammed with passengers and crowd estimates throughout the night and the following day ranged from 50,000 upwards. They swarmed all over the Flats and lined the bridges above, seeking the best available vantage points. Seventy policemen were needed to control the surging mob, and a terrible accident was miraculously avoided when a spectator-covered lumber pile shifted, pitching dozens of rubberneckers onto more gawkers below.

One by one, the bleeding, muddy, broken corpses were fished out of the river and taken to one of six private morgues. Owing to the competitive relations among the latter, disgraceful scenes occurred as rival morgue employees fought each other and even grieving relatives for possession of the bodies. One such macabre episode was the recovery of the body of Miss Martha Sauernheimer, as recounted by a *Plain Dealer* reporter:

> Friends telephoned for an ambulance, and in a short time two of Heffron's and Hogan and Sharar's appeared. Heffron's arrived first, and his men made a rush for the body. As they neared the edge of the pier they were seized by the brother and brother-in-law of the dead girl, and commanded not to touch the body. They tried to shake the enraged relatives off, and quite a little struggle ensued. Young Sauernheimer said that he had given orders to Undertaker Mattmueller to come for the body, and any other person would touch it at his peril.

It was only after another hour, while thousands gawked at the bleeding, bedraggled corpse that Mattmueller's ambulance arrived and bore off poor Miss Martha's body.

With the last known corpse, that of Matthew Callihan, recovered at 2:15 on Monday afternoon, November 18, two tasks now provided further diversion to expectant Clevelanders. First came the funerals of the deceased—seven of them on Tuesday alone—pathetic spectacles all reported in every sobbing detail by Cleveland's daily newspapers. Prizes for most bathetic media coverage and disgraceful conduct went to, respectively, the *Plain Dealer* and the spectators at the Hoffman family funeral. Mrs. Annie Hoffman, 30, had been on #642 with her son Harry, 7, and daughter

Gertrude, 4. All journalistic stops were pulled out for the wake at the Hoffman home at 1508 Pearl Street in paragraphs that put Dickens's description of Little Nell's demise to shame:

> The funeral obsequies held over this mother and her two babes were sad. Sad because of their simplicity, infinitely sad because of the grief of the only survivor of the little family. In the modest home on Pearl Street the three sleeping forms were laid out in caskets of purest white. On the right reposed the little, golden haired girl, her features as beautiful as an angel's, nestling in its satin pillow, while the ringlets of gold fell round the face, making a halo which completed a picture of the rarest beauty. On the left the body reclined, a few red scars—mute witnesses of the awful calamity—marring the otherwise peaceful expression of his face. And in the middle the mother slept— slumbering in eternal sleep, while on her face also naught but happiness was to be read—happiness in eternity with her children! Glancing from those sleeping forms to the beautiful floral offerings, only a sharper pang shot through one's heart. There was a beautiful design of "Gates Ajar," with two large, white floral gates standing half open, waiting to receive the spirits of the dead: an anchor surmounted by a dove of purest white told of hope and peace; a harp with a broken string of a life departed.

Hundreds of ghoulish spectators turned the Hoffman funerals into a shameful spectacle. When the crush at the entrance of St. Paul's Church became so great as to require the intervention of the police, the frustrated mob made a frantic rush for the rear entrance of the church. While the morbidly curious filed past the three open caskets—some of them two, three, or more times—others fought, fidgeted, and elbowed in the aisles and staircases until their din could be heard above the peal of the church organ.

Other victims of the viaduct horror were an interesting cross-section of Cleveland's turn-of-the-century population. Miss Bessie Davies, 22, was a second-grade school teacher at the Sackett Street

School, assistant Sunday school librarian, and enthusiastic member of the Scranton Avenue Free Baptist Church. She was returning from a visit to her uncle on the East Side and on her way to Saturday night choir practice when she met her fate.

Henry Mecklenburg, 35, was a tailor, easily identified at his autopsy by the packet of needles in his pocket and his right clubfoot. Unmarried, he had lived with his mother and sister and had only been in the United States for a few years.

Marie Nettgen, 22, had been visiting her brother that Saturday afternoon. A domestic servant, she had emigrated to the U.S. about 1890, and was a devout member of St. Michael's Church on Scranton Avenue.

Minnie Brown, 40, was head cook at the Broadway Cafe on St. Clair, near the Cleveland Theater. Married twice, she had been recently widowed for the second time and left with five children. Her son Daniel, 15, when called upon to identify her corpse at McGarry's Morgue, could only sob, "My God, it is my mother. And there are four children depending on me for support!" Minnie's autopsy revealed a fractured skull and she rests to this day in an obscure corner of Riverside Cemetery, beneath a humble stone labeled simply "Mama."

James McLaughlin also sleeps in Riverside, amid a plot occupied by family and in-laws. Mildly less obscure than the other victims, McLaughlin, a union printer by trade, was known around Cleveland as an excellent amateur baseball pitcher and had pitched a year of professional ball in the old American Association. Examination of his body at McGarry's morgue disclosed a fractured skull, a broken neck, and much broken glass ground into his clothing. There was $1.10 in his pockets, two memoranda books, buttons, and two keys. He would have celebrated his 35th birthday on Monday, November 18.

Louis Hueltz, 28, was a well-liked U.S. mail carrier on his West Side route. Diver Walter Metcalf had to cut his body in two to get it out from under the trolley wheels at the bottom of the river. He left a wife and two children.

Car #642 races toward Death.

Curt LePhene was only 15. The son of a German army officer, he had immigrated to Cleveland just the previous month, when his widowed mother came here to be with her new husband. When hauled out of the Cuyahoga he was wearing an overcoat and vest, a checked brown coat, and trousers.

Harry Foster, 19, had been a timekeeper in the millinery department at Root & McBride's Bank Street (West 6th) store for the previous 18 months. Identified by a card on his body, Harry, whose skull was crushed by the accident, was on his way home from a football game at Oberlin when death took him. By sheer luck, the catastrophe spared his acquaintance, Mark L. Thompsen, who had also attended the same game. Although both had returned to

Cleveland via the Erie Railroad, only Harry had won the footrace to make the 7:30 car at Broadway & Ontario.

One of the sadder casualties was Mrs. Martha Palmer, 59, of 165 Kenilworth Street in the Flats. Abandoned by her husband in 1886, she had struggled to make a living as a dressmaker since. Her daughter Lida broke down completely while identifying her mother's body at the morgue: "Oh Mama, can't you speak to me? If you could only speak one word. She can't hear me—she is dead!"

The official inquest into the Viaduct disaster opened at 9 a.m. on Tuesday, November 19. Hundreds of spectators were packed into the coroner's courtroom. Like virtually all inquests following Cleveland disasters during the last century, it opened with high expectations and closed with muttered, inconclusive, and harmless recriminations. The chief witness was motorman Augustus Rogers. He adamantly denied any knowledge that the electrical cut-off had been inoperative and he insisted that there were no red warning lights, either on the safety gates or posted above. About a dozen eyewitnesses subsequently gave conflicting testimony about the warning lights, leaving the question moot. A shattered red lantern was recovered from the depths of the Cuyahoga—but unfriendly rumor had it that parties friendly to Bridge Captain Brenner or interests sensitive to the potential liability of Big Con in the disaster had thrown several similar lanterns into the river after the fact. While Cleveland City Council debated blustering and thoroughly silly legislation to prevent similar disasters, the inquest shuddered to its predictable conclusion, given its many hours of irreconcilable and even incomprehensible testimony. Or as the *Cleveland Press* cynically summarized matters:

> The testimony brought out before the coroner regarding the Central Viaduct accident indicates that people may see strange things when they are frightened. Some of the witnesses have declared that they saw red lights upon the safety gates; others say that they saw white lights upon the gates, and others are positive that there were no lights of any color. Other witnesses

> have sworn that the gates were shut; still others have testified that the gates were open, and some of the people who claim to have been upon the spot at the time of the accident are positive that no one who stood more than 50 feet away from the draw could have seen whether the gates were shut or not. It has also been asserted before the coroner that a lighted lantern was thrown into the river several minutes after the accident occurred; and one witness asserted upon oath that he knew that a lantern found in the river two or three days after the accident was the one.

The final verdict, delivered by Coroner George W. Arbuckle on December 9 satisfied no one, except perhaps the officials of Big Con. Arbuckle's judgment was that no one involved in the accident had technically committed an "unlawful act," so his finding was that no one was to blame.

More decisive action, however, had already been taken on other fronts. On the Monday morning, November 18, some "Big Con" employees showed up at the viaduct and installed a new electrical cutoff. And when another disaster almost occurred on the Superior Viaduct on November 22, Little Con officials in charge responded immediately. With three streetcars waiting at the western end of Superior draw at 2 a.m., several of the motormen had left their cars to gossip with each other. The rearmost car, driverless, suddenly bumped the next car, which in turn pushed the front car toward the draw. It stopped just a foot short of the safety gate, and Motorman R. A. Dittrick and Conductor R. R. Patterson were subsequently fired for leaving their vehicles.

The later history of the Central Viaduct was not a happy one. The draw span was removed in 1912, and replaced with a high level truss-bridge that eliminated the draw entirely. One of the worst fires in Cleveland history, the Fisher-Wilson lumber conflagration on May 25, 1914, destroyed 300 feet of the viaduct. It was rebuilt but became increasingly unsafe and hard to maintain as the years went by. Upkeep problems, as with the Superior Viaduct, were aggravated by continual sinking of the land under its western approaches. The opening of the Lorain-Carnegie Bridge in 1932 obviated much of the need for the Central Viaduct, and it was finally closed and condemned in 1941. During World War II it was razed, and its 500 tons of metal were converted into scrap metal. All that remains today are a few of its stone supporting piers on both sides of the river and several yards of its old trolley tracks, which can yet be seen in the street just south of the eastern end of the Lorain-Carnegie bridge. That, and a copy of an 1895 ballad whose eighth and last stanza contains the last words on the Central Viaduct Disaster:

> The bridgeman claimed he did the work and he was not to
>   blame.
> But someone must be punished or it will occur again.
> Who the guilty party is it's not for me to say.
> But God above will point him out upon the Judgment Day.

# DAMN THE TORPEDOES

## The Fireworks Factory Horrors (1902–1903)

The 1908 S. S. Kresge fireworks explosion disaster is one of Cleveland's most poignant and celebrated disasters. In the century since it occurred, Clevelanders have taken justifiable pride in the impetus that tragedy gave to the "Safe and Sane Fourth of July" movement that eventually curtailed the annual carnage of American patriotic celebrations. Less well known, however, and less of a credit to the repute of the Forest City, is the story of the 1902 and 1903 torpedo factory explosions. Taken together, they killed and injured more persons and wreaked far more property damage than the 1908 dime store horror. Sadly, much as their stories are now forgotten, their lessons at the time were ignored, in a civic amnesia that made the 1908 horror almost inevitable. The story of the torpedo disasters provides yet more brutal evidence that the Forest City has had a very slow learning curve when it comes to protecting its citizens.

What was once the southwest corner of the intersection of Euclid Avenue and Fairmount Street is today but a modernistic component of the ever-expanding Cleveland Clinic campus. But in the spring of 1902 it was the site occupied by the Fairmount Manufacturing Company. Situated on the second floor over quarters occupied by the De Mars Bicycle Shop, the Fairmount Company factory consisted of a molding room fronting on Euclid Avenue, a mixing room in the center, and a storeroom at the rear. Communication with the street was by a rickety staircase, and all the second-floor windows but one were nailed shut with strips of wood. True, there was a "fire escape" adjacent to the one unbarred window. Some fussy Cleveland city building inspector had insisted on that after a couple of previous, if inconsequential explosions at the Fairmount. What it was, in fact, was a flimsy wooden ladder nailed nearly flat against the side of the building. Not exactly the recourse one might wish if one were fleeing from a burning torpedo factory.

In 1902, a "torpedo" was exactly what the *Oxford English Dictionary* still defines as "a toy consisting of fulminating powder and fine gravel wrapped in thin paper, which explodes when thrown on a hard surface." There was great demand for torpedoes in that era of unregulated fireworks, and Fairmount Company owner-manager R. H. Opes and his crew of 16 women (mostly teenaged girls) and eight men had been working feverishly since the factory opened in March to meet the expected July Fourth demand. It was hard work with long hours, to be sure, but no worse than the lot of most working-class Clevelanders of the era. And, as owner-manager Opes constantly reassured his employees, the torpedoes were not dangerous, since they contained neither nitroglycerin nor dynamite, the only explosive substances prohibited by law in the densely populated residential neighborhood in which the Fairmount was situated.

It happened just after work began at 7 a.m. on Saturday, March 15. The regular mixer of the critical torpedo formula was late, so chemist Frank Groch recruited 18-year-old Will Fisher to mix the starter mixture of potash and sulfur in a bowl. Fisher was new to the task, so Groch was careful to warn him about creating sparks by stirring too vigorously. Apparently, Groch wasn't careful enough. Several minutes after 7:00 a spark ignited the contents of Fisher's bowl. Attempting to carry it out of the mixing room, he spilled some of it into a barrel of volatile chemicals, principally sulfur. Seconds later, the barrel exploded, filling the second floor with flying debris, suffocating chemical fumes, and the screams of panicked employees. An instant later, flames sprang up, fed by the residue of

**Explosion Kills One and Injures Many in Factory of Explosives**

**Terrible Struggles of the Working People to Get From the Windows Which Were Barred Up--Grand Jury Will Fix Responsibility**

*Cleveland World*, March 15, 1902.

sawdust and gunpowder on the floor. Chemist Groch made it out of the room just in time. With a dazed Will Fisher at his heels, he fled toward the rear, screaming, "Run for your lives! The building is all afire."

The torpedo workers in the middle and rear rooms escaped fairly quickly and easily by means of the tumbledown staircase. But the fire and the suffocating clouds of chemical smoke that attacked their lungs and made it impossible to see anything in the choking inferno of the second floor immediately trapped the dozen workers left in the front molding room. Eyewitness Walter Moffet, a trolley conductor, was passing by in his streetcar when he saw the building in flames. He immediately abandoned his car, grabbed a ladder, and climbed to the barred windows. He would remember what he saw through the nailed wooden slats for the rest of his life:

> It was an awful sight. The girls were pushing their arms through the windows and tearing at the wooden bars. Blood flowed from the cuts and their shrieks for help were heartrending. The hair on their heads was afire and they were trying to protect their faces and force the bars from the window at the same time.

That any of those trapped in the molding room were saved was owing to the heroism of several men. One was H. Gunthrie, a clerk at a nearby drugstore. He climbed the "fire escape," broke a window open and managed to pull two girls out through the opening. Fireman C. A. Spillman, who arrived with Engine Company 18 from the Doan Street station, got up a ladder in time to rescue Elizabeth Cotrell and her sister Lena Karpp, both of them badly burned. Several of the other workers who survived managed to leap unhurt from the broken windows before being overcome by smoke.

The entire explosion/fire sequence lasted no more than 10 minutes. When firemen finally smashed their way into the molding room, they found Anna Fritz, 17, dead from suffocation and atrociously burnt. Christina Schnitzer, 16, and Kittie Howard, 18, were taken out alive to Charity Hospital, but Christina died 20 hours later and Kittie succumbed to burns and sulfur inhalation at 7:30 a.m. on Tuesday morning. Anna Fritz had only been on the job two days, and Kittie had started work just that morning. There were seven serious injuries in addition to the three Fairmount deaths.

The subsequent official investigation did credit to no one. Owner-manager Opes denied under oath that there had been any explosion and insisted that it was only a fire. Investigating officer Cleveland Police captain Fred Kohler waxed eloquent on the infamy of the Fairmount factory, fulminating that it was a "sweatshop" where the "girls were packed in like sardines." But his opinion that the factory was simply a "deathtrap" did not preclude his agreeing with the ultimate finding of the official inquest, which found the Fairmount Company in violation of no existing laws and blameless for the events of March 15.

Apparently, nothing was learned from the Fairmount disaster. True, R. H. Opes's torpedo concern ceased operations, but that was due only to his completely uninsured $10,000 loss on the factory. Nothing was done by the city of Cleveland—much less the Ohio legislature—either to forbid the operation of torpedo factories in residential neighborhoods or to tighten restrictions on their use of inflammable or explosive materials. So when the next spring

THE DEAD GIRL AND OTHER VICTIMS OF THE FIRE.

Victims of the Fairmount torpedo fire.
*Cleveland Press*, March 15, 1902.

rolled around there were three torpedo factories running full tilt in Cleveland. One was the Crescent Appliance Company on Case Avenue (East 40th Street) near St. Clair; the second was on Berlin Street (West 81st) near Madison Avenue. But the largest and most dangerous factory was the Thor Manufacturing Company at 647 Orange Street just a few steps from Case Avenue.

Owned by Joseph Raquett and Silas Cole, the Thor torpedo factory was a two-story wooden frame building, extending 60 feet back from the street and facing south on Orange Street. The concern employed eight women and seven men (mostly teenagers), plus managing owner Raquett and Cole's son Wilbur. The red, white, and blue torpedo "canes" that constituted the factory's chief product were small but noisy fireworks especially prized by small children too young for more powerful holiday armament. Owner Raquett would later claim there were no more than 100 pounds of dangerous materials—chiefly sulfur and potash—in the building, and he may have been correct. But the first floor was filled with boxes of finished torpedoes awaiting shipment, and the second-floor mixing area was covered with sawdust and accumulated powder debris from the torpedo mixture. The previous year, after several minor explosions at the Thor factory, John W. Bath, the state inspector of workshops, had ordered company officials to change the sawdust every two days to prevent dangerous buildup—but Raquett and Cole had failed to implement his order. Given the indifference of the Thor management to the safety of its employees and the location of the factory in the most densely populated area of Cleveland, all was in place for an unprecedented Forest City tragedy.

It came on Saturday, May 2, at exactly 12:16 p.m. The tragedy began as a practical joke. No one working with the flammable torpedo mixture was allowed to wear shoes in the second-floor mixing area. But Gusta Wolf, eating her lunch in an adjacent area, was wearing her shoes when a new employee, Mary Hollenen, gave her a playful shove. As Wolf slid across the floor into the sawdust, her shoes struck a spark. A second later, a flame sprang up, fed by the torpedo residue on the floor. Wolf quickly threw a basin of water on the blaze, but it was already too late. Joseph Katz, a laborer working on a new house next door to the factory, saw the developing scene through an open window. He screamed, "Run for your lives!" and immediately set the example. Smoke began to pour out of the windows, and within seconds the Thor building exits were streaming with panicked, fleeing employees.

Ironically, the Thor workers suffered relatively less than persons in neighboring houses or just passersby, because the initial fire provided sufficient warning for them to escape. But with the exception of the lucky Joseph Katz, the rest of the people in the crowded neighborhood had had no warning whatsoever when the contents of the Thor shipping room exploded at exactly 12:16 p.m.

It was the largest explosion in Cleveland history up to that time, and still probably the second-largest after the 1944 East Ohio Gas Company blast. It pulverized the Thor factory and a dozen adjoining houses and damaged hundreds of others within a half-mile radius. It damaged storefronts and residences for a half-mile stretch on both Orange and Woodland Avenues and knocked virtually everyone flat in that square mile of Cleveland. It smashed practically every pane of glass within 3,000 feet of the factory and was felt as far away as Doan Street (East 105th) and in Public Square.

The worst of it was in the new residential development just west and to the rear of the factory. Built by developer E. Brudno and leased mostly to Jewish families, the half-dozen or so homes took the brunt of the blast. Most were completely demolished, leaving but a precarious partition or single exterior wall in grotesque silhouette. The three deaths in the disaster occurred in the Morris Cohen residence, just 12 feet to the west of the Thor factory. Cohen had just brought his family of eight over from England to his new house the previous Monday, and the explosion caught his wife and two of his sons at their midday meal. Firemen quickly pulled the three of them from the splintered ruins of the house, but Mrs. Cohen bled to death from a severed neck artery in an ambulance on the way to the hospital. Five hours later, her son Solly, 12, died of a fractured skull at St. Vincent Charity Hospital, followed four hours afterward by Benjamin, 18, who had lost the top of his head in the explosion.

Another house hard hit was the Barney Quass residence directly behind the Thor factory. Mrs. Quass ended up in the hospital with her badly injured daughter Mabel and son Harry. They were joined there by Mamie Meyer, 14, of 1265 Case Avenue, whose left eye was taken out by flying glass and Wilbur Cole, son of the Thor co-owner, found bruised, cut, and horribly lacerated under the factory ruins. Many of the wounded had simply been walking in the area when the wave of the blast knocked them off their feet. Every ambulance

Buildings destroyed by the Thor explosion. *Cleveland Leader*, May 3, 1903.

in Cleveland was soon busy handling the casualties that jammed area hospitals through the weekend.

The Thor catastrophe produced the usual anomalies and heroics peculiar to such disasters. Mrs. Morris Weingarten was sitting in her rocking chair in the parlor at 12634 Case Avenue when the blast flipped her and the chair into a complete somersault. Miss Annie Sandrowsky of 1290 Case Avenue was so traumatized by the explosion that, although physically uninjured, she lost the power of speech. More inspiring was the experience of Arthur and Lizzie Conroy, Thor employees who were brother and sister. Lizzie escaped the burning building, only to go back inside to find her missing brother. Arthur, in fact, had also escaped, but he saw her reenter and risked his life to bring her back out again. They were just a few feet away from the factory when it exploded and knocked them senseless—but left them alive.

Amazingly, the final butcher's bill was only three dead and a couple of hundred injured. Unamazingly, the official sequel to the Thor tragedy followed the familiar script of public bravado and masterly inaction. Cleveland newspaper editorials shrieked loudly for punishment of the responsible parties and demanded an end to such lethal establishments in residential neighborhoods. Cuyahoga County coroner Thomas A. Burke, for his part, promised, "Someone is to blame and I expect to find out who it is." But his inquest, which commenced as the Cohen dead were tearfully buried in Fre-

A group of survivors of the explosion, *Cleveland Leader*, May 2, 1903.

mont Cemetery and squads of police battled small boys searching for unexploded torpedoes in the Thor ruins, proved to be the usual empty civic ritual. Although Dr. Perry Hobbs of Western Reserve University testified that the torpedo mixture used was nearly as efficient as nitroglycerin as an explosive agent, Burke could not find any law prohibiting its use in city factories. True, state inspector of explosives Bath did bring up that little matter of his ignored order about exchanging the sawdust on the mixing floor, but he, County Prosecutor Harvey Keeler, and Coroner Burke agreed that it was too "technical" a violation of state law to pursue. Six days after the explosion, Burke issued his verdict, which was that the Thor explosion was purely "accidental" and that he held no one responsible.

The lesson of the second torpedo tragedy was not entirely lost on the city. On May 8, Cleveland fire chief George A. Wallace ordered the closure of the city's remaining torpedo factories. No more lives were lost or homes imperiled in the manufacture of "harmless" fireworks within the Cleveland city limits. But no one articulated the next logical step, which was to prohibit the storage of large amounts of explosive material in areas used by the public. Thus, the stage was set for the memorable tragedy of July 3, 1908, the last of Cleveland's three fireworks horrors. (For details of that disaster, see the chapter "Cleveland's Saddest Fourth.")

# CLEVELAND'S SADDEST CIRCUS DAY

## The Ringling Brothers and Barnum & Bailey Fire

## (1942)

Few spectacles are harder to endure than that of a brute animal in pain. Although largely forgotten now, the 1942 Ringling Brothers and Barnum & Bailey Circus fire in Cleveland was replete with a multitude of such dreadful sights, and they remained etched in the memories of the circus folk, spectators, and Cleveland firemen who witnessed them. Even worse, lessons learned from the tragic blaze went unheeded, as the even more catastrophic Hartford, Connecticut, circus fire—in which 168 persons died—would demonstrate only two years later.

August 4, 1942, was a fine, sunny day in Cleveland. The Ringling Brothers Circus was in its second day of a four-day, eight-show stint at the circus grounds on the north side of Lakeside at East 9th. Boasting 1,009 animals and 800 performers, and specially redesigned by Norman Bel Geddes and George Balanchine, the circus brought welcome cheer to Clevelanders caught up in the toils, tears, and anxiety of World War II. It was nearing noon, and many of the circus folk were sleeping, while others prepared themselves and the animals for the 2:15 performance.

The tragedy happened at about 11:45 a.m. A pile of straw at

Aftermath of fire, circus grounds, East 9th Street and Lakeside Avenue.

the west end of the menagerie tent suddenly erupted in crackling flames. Quickly reaching the paraffin- and benzene- coated tent, the flames raced the length of the tent in mere seconds, fed by the straw bedding of the caged animals and the hay, straw, and feed stockpiled around the tent.

It was all over, except for the suffering, in just 15 minutes. Many of the animals, such as two of the giraffes, two tigers, and a pair of lions, were simply "cooked" in their cages. Ten camels, tethered together, were trapped in place and died where they stood. A herd of zebras, many of them badly burned, fled in panic toward the railroad tracks just north of the circus grounds. When two companies of Cleveland firemen and a high-pressure unit finally got the fire out, 65 animals lay dead or dying on the Ringling lot. And it could have been worse: only a favorable wind and frantic efforts by firefighters prevented the blaze from engulfing the adjacent horse tent and its 160 horses. The only humans injured were the elephant boss, who was burned, and another employee who was accidentally clipped with an elephant hook in the afternoon's turmoil.

Most pitiful were the elephants. Four of them were terribly burned, some of the ears completely burned off, with the folds of their skin hanging in charred fragments. Highly disciplined, the elephants had refused to leave the flaming tent until Walter McClain, the elephant boss, came to lead them away.

Rosie, the pachyderm with a "bad" reputation, died first. Maddened by pain and repeatedly breaking restraining chains, she ran amok until police detective Lloyd Trunk, acting on orders of circus veterinarian J. J. Henderson, put a bullet between her eyes, and policeman D. L. Cowles emptied a submachine gun into her side. Several hours later, Ringling Rose, her pelt completely burnt off, suffered the same fate. The two remaining elephants, Trilby and Cass, were taken to the basement of Public Hall, where they and the other burned animals were tenderly painted with a special burn salve, "Follie," flown in from New York. Trilby died at midnight, and Cass expired early that same morning.

Ten of the victims were camels. Veterinarian Henderson tried to save another three of them—Pasha, En Route, and Tillie—but Detective Trunk finally had to end their sufferings, too, with 9 or 10 bullets apiece. Dr. Henderson remembered their deaths this way: "They lay down, staring out off into space like old men looking out of a club window, and died." The final death toll included 4 lions, 3 tigers, 2 giraffes, 12 zebras, 1 ostrich, 3 pumas, 16 monkeys, 2 black bucks, 1 sacred Indian cow, and 13 camels. The corpses of the dead animals were taken to the Stadler Products Company, a rendering plant on Denison Avenue.

William O. Walker of the *Call & Post* gave the best eyewitness account of the fire. He was close enough to see the first sheet of flame erupt, and he eloquently described the unspeakable sights he saw that day: "The most awesome aspect of the tragic spectacle was the complete silence of the animals. No agonizing screams, no anguished roars. Just silence inside the tent, with the crackle of flames

Smoky debris from menagerie tent fire.

outside." Later, he wrote of his anguished tour of the smoking ruins: "All about the ringed circle, where, only a few minutes before, had stood one of the finest menageries in the world, were the smoldering cages. Inside these cages were lions, leopards, and other beasts of the cat family, all burned, but not dead. In agony, they moved on feet bleeding from burns, and stared into space through eyes that no longer had vision. It was indeed a heart-rending sight . . ."

The cause of the $200,000 blaze, which was not covered by insurance, was never proven. Two days after the fire, the Allegheny County, Pennsylvania, police picked up a 16-year-old drifter named Lemadris Ford, a native of Pittsburgh, who readily confessed that he and a friend named "Jeff" had set the fire in revenge for being fired from the circus just hours before the blaze. According to Ford, they had chugged a bottle of wine, returned to the menagerie tent, and thrown lighted cigarettes onto the straw. They then fled Cleveland by hopping on a convenient freight train—but only after collecting their back wages at 5 p.m. that day. Cleveland police detectives, however, found severe inconsistencies in Ford's "confession"

Circus employees in bucket brigade.

and decided he was either seeking notoriety or suffering from hallucinations. Which left either the possibility of a carelessly thrown cigarette (by either a circus worker or spectator) or even sparks from a train on the tracks just north of the Lakeside circus grounds. Historical accounts of the tragedy list the cause of the 1942 fire as "unknown." What is definitely known is that the proper lesson was not drawn from the tragedy: two years later 168 people in an identical tent waterproofed with paraffin and benzene would die in another circus fire in Hartford, Connecticut.

The show went on again that evening and afterwards, its presenters undeterred by the catastrophe, especially as most of the animals killed had not performed in the Big Ring. But John Ringling

North, the circus chief, best expressed the fire's impact when he spoke for all the circus folk that terrible day: "I can stand the loss incurred in the fire, but I just cannot stand to have the animals suffer." His sentiments were poignantly echoed by head animal handler John Sabo, who had worked with the Ringling Circus since 1915: "I would rather lose my right arm than to see something like this happen. I like them all like babies. I felt like bawling when I found out that Maggie and Mabel (the brindled gnus) had died."

# DEATH RIDE AT EUCLID BEACH

## The Sad Fate of Joseph Senk (1943)

Cleveland's amusement parks have furnished an ample portion of Cleveland woe. Their most persistent nemesis has been fire. Euclid Beach Park's movie theater burned down in 1908, and the nearby White City Amusement Park was razed by fire in 1906 before its final destruction during a violent storm two years later. Puritas Springs Park was visited by devastating fires in 1910 and 1946. And Luna Park was hit by serious blazes in 1908, 1927, 1929, and 1938. (The 1908 fire destroyed its popular "Human Dry Cleaner" ride, a revolving barrel that, like Euclid Beach's later "Flying Turns," caused its male and female occupants to become delightfully entangled.)

Such mishaps have not been entirely unexpected. It's no secret, of course, that much of the enduring appeal of amusement parks has always been the genuine but controlled terror generated by their "rides." And no ride in Cleveland history was more terrifying—and thus beloved—than the Euclid Beach Park "Thriller," the unchallenged king of area roller coasters for almost half a century. Designed by the Philadelphia Toboggan Company and erected during the winter of 1923–1924, the Thriller enraptured generations of Clevelanders with its breakneck speed and high (71 feet, 5 inches!) elevations. Built for $90,000, it paid for itself in one season and was undisputedly the most popular attraction at Euclid Beach until

The summit of all Cleveland fears: the "Thriller" in action.

the park's 1969 demise. Boasting three trains in nonstop rotation during its salad days, a Thriller unit was composed of three cars with four seats each. Many an aging Clevelander can recall both the exhilaration of its ride and the chilling rumors that clung to its creaky wooden structure. Truly, a Euclid Beach visit was not complete until the inevitable moment an impressionable youngster was told to be careful because "a boy once stood up on the Thriller and fell off and was killed." How terrifying to a child! How scary even to a cautious adult! And . . . how deeply pleasurable!

The remarkable thing about such minatory folktales is that they contained a kernel of truth. There *were* two serious accidents on the Thriller, and one of them cost the life of an imprudent 16-year-old boy. The first mishap occurred sometime in the 1920s, probably in

1 Killed, 8 Injured on Roller Coasters

Youth Dies in Plunge From Euclid Beach's "Thriller"

*Cleveland Press*, July 5, 1943.

the coaster's early years before its second hill was severely reduced in height. An unidentified boy stood up in a car as a train rounded the final curve. Someone tickled him from behind, causing him to catapult out of the train, bounce off the guardrail and three high tension wires, and then to carom off several branches of an adjacent sycamore tree. He landed badly bruised and shaken, but alive.

The second, fatal, and well-documented episode happened shortly before midnight on July 3, 1943. East Technical High School student Joseph Senk, 16, began horsing around in the front seat of a Thriller lead car the moment it left the station and began climbing that first, rackety monster hill. Twice he stood up as the train was whipped above the tracks by its momentum, and twice his companion, William Troscht, 17, pulled him back down in his seat.

Troscht didn't get a third chance. As Senk stood up a third time on the Thriller's final turn, he was hurled from the car in an instant. A second later his head smashed into the guardrail posts at the side of the tracks, and he was probably lying dead there by the time his train pulled into its station. All of the passengers on the train except for Troscht quickly dispersed into the anonymous crowd, and Euclid Beach Park personnel and Cleveland safety officials were left with little testimony as to exactly how the tragedy had occurred. It's even probable that none of the other riders on the train, save Troscht, were aware of what had happened. It looked like a simple case of sheer youthful folly, and probers were soon more interested in what caused a crash that injured eight persons on the park's "Aero Dip" ride the next day.

Senk's funeral was held in St. Casimir Church on July 7, and he lies buried in Calvary Cemetery. The day before his final rites, Cuyahoga County coroner Samuel Gerber ruled his death an accident, finding no fault with either the *Thriller's* mechanics or the Euclid Beach Park management.

# CLEVELAND'S BURNING!

## A Trio of Catastrophic Fires (1883–1914)

It's an unkind irony that Cleveland's best-known fire is the 1969 Cuyahoga River blaze that made national headlines and was eventually immortalized in a Randy Newman song. It wasn't the first time the Cuyahoga caught on fire, and it certainly wasn't its most serious or expensive combustion. And it couldn't hold a candle to at least a half dozen fires that have actually threatened Cleveland's very existence as a city during its two centuries. Perhaps the most catastrophic were the great fires of 1883, 1884, and 1914.

### The First Terror of Kingsbury Run: The 1883 Standard Oil Fire

As the *Plain Dealer* later remarked, 1883 did not augur well for the world. Zadkiel Tao Sze's *London Almanac*, which had been published since 1831, predicted "all manner of calamities by flood, fire, crime and war." Raphael, a London astrologer since 1821, also predicted unprecedented troubles, warning especially of catastrophes for "mercantile interests." Sadly, before the year was through, Cleveland was to get more than its usual share of such woes.

Cleveland was already in a state of emergency by Friday, February 2. Rising temperatures combined with torrential rains began to melt accumulated snow and ice that morning and by Saturday had produced the worst floods in Cleveland history. Most of the Flats and the Cuyahoga River Valley all the way from the Superior Viaduct south to Broadway were inundated with five or more feet of water. Much railroad rolling stock was under water, many bridges were badly damaged, and from 20 to 25 million feet of lumber from Flats lumberyards was floating out to Lake Erie and oblivion. Two men were drowned, and the total commercial losses from the floods alone were probably $1.5 million even before a more dangerous enemy—fire—struck on Saturday morning.

It began at the Shurmer & Teagle Refinery just west of Willson Avenue (now East 55th). Waste oil from a Standard Oil facility upstream on Kingsbury Run had been leaking for some hours, helping to swell the normally two-foot-deep Run into a raging, oily torrent. Surging past the boiler house of the Shurmer works adjacent to the Run, the oil was ignited by falling coals. Kingsbury Run burst into flames, and the greatest fire in Cleveland history was under way.

The first alarm was called in from Box 69 at 6:20 a.m. Saturday, and Engine Companies 7, 9, and 13, as well as Truck 3, responded. Within several hours, the blaze had spread to the Merriam & Morgan paraffin works downstream, at which point Box 56 called in Engine Companies 3 and 8 and reactivated Companies 7 and 13, and Truck 3. Despite the best efforts of the firemen, thousands of gallons of burning oil continued to pour into the Run. Just about the time firemen got the Shurmer & Teagle blaze under control, the stream of burning oil reached the main Standard Oil works, three miles downstream.

There was, undoubtedly, a terrible beauty to the destruction that waxed over the next 24 hours. Thousands of Clevelanders, estimated at half its 180,000 population, witnessed it, many of them vigorously obstructing the efforts of firemen. All streetcars to the area and the local saloons were jammed by the curious. The Standard Oil stills and tanks, filled with gasoline, coal oil, petroleum, and tar, began to explode and burn about 12:30 p.m. Through the still-driving rain, dense black smoke and arcing flames began to

FOURTH EDITION.

FURIOUS FLAMES!!!!

THE FIRE-FIEND ATTACKS THE STANDARD.

Fast Floating Fire Followed by the Most Terrific Explosions.

TANK AFTER TANK, STILL AFTER STILL BLOWS UP, AND THE END IS NOT YET.

*Cleveland Press* headline, February 3, 1883.

fill the horizon of Cleveland. One by one, nine enormous Standard Oil storage tanks, each containing from five to 16,000 barrels of oil, kerosene, or gasoline, blew up over the next 12 hours, adding thousands of additional, lethal gallons to the inflammable torrent rushing toward downtown Cleveland. At one point, no fewer than seven oil tanks were burning at once.

If ever Cleveland came close to the fate of Chicago in 1871, it was on the afternoon of February 3. Fire Chief James W. Dickinson, who arose from a feverish sickbed to orchestrate the smoke-eating heroics, later recalled waiting for one of the 16,000-barrel oil tanks to explode:

> Cowen [head of the Standard Oil safety forces] said to me that when it became necessary I should wave my hat and the Standard's fire department would open out on the tank. I looked up and saw that the tank was boiling over and all ready for the grand collapse, and said, "well, they had better begin now." At

> that instant the tank boiled over with a blinding flash, but the Standard firemen didn't wait to begin . . . You see a tank usually boils about five hours after it takes fire before the grand blow-out occurs, and one can tell pretty nearly when the explosion is to take place.

As at Gettysburg, the fate of the city turned on a simple railroad embankment, adjacent to an obstructed culvert by Broadway Avenue. As the flaming river of fire moved closer and closer to that culvert, Cleveland firemen realized that if they didn't stop it there it would jump downstream to ignite both sides of the Flats all the way to the mouth of the Cuyahoga. It was a time for heroes, and Cleveland's firefighters did not disappoint. The climax came early Sunday morning, as reported by the *Cleveland Leader*:

> As on Saturday, the great fight was to keep the fire from getting across or under the NYP & O bridge and into the purifying works [filled with gasoline] on the side of the Cuyahoga River. Yet the warfare was a triangular one. To the north of the flames stood forty ponderous tanks filled with crude oil, and standing so thickly together as to give that vicinity the name of 'Tanktown.' The fire was in momentary danger of reaching these great storehouses yet unharmed. To the east were the extensive Doan works that were guarded by three engines, while the great objective point was the river. Had the fire once jumped across the embankment that runs between Kingsbury Run and the Cuyahoga, no one can estimate what it might have done.

Concentrating their blasts on the embankment, Cleveland firemen and Standard Oil's own safety forces battled for hours to keep the flaming torrent of Kingsbury Run from jumping north of Broadway and the New York, Pennsylvania & Ohio railroad tracks. Many of them spent hours waist deep in the icy, oil-drenched waters of Kingsbury Run. At one point a flaming stream of naphtha did escape to the other side—but it was beaten back by the exhausted, scorched, and seared men. Many Cleveland firemen spent up to 50 hours battling the three-day fire.

By early Sunday morning, the city had been saved, but exhausted firemen continued to pour water on the various blazes well into Monday. By the time the conflagration was finished, late Monday evening, February 5, nine large storage tanks, 30 stills, and other Standard Oil facilities were in ruins, not to mention the hundreds of thousands of gallons of petroleum products lost. The total losses to Standard Oil were estimated between $250,000 and $300,000, with losses to other businesses totaling about $500,000. Miraculously, there were no fatalities, despite many fire-related injuries, especially to Cleveland firemen.

Although some improvements were subsequently made to the Cleveland Fire Department's equipment, later and yet more terrible fires in 1884 would give evidence that the lessons of the 1883 Standard Oil fire had not been learned. As Chief Dickinson remarked, just two days after the final flames were extinguished: "The citizens of Cleveland will never know how near the city came to burning up. But for the protection formed by the NYPO track the burning oil would have run down the culvert and out into the river."

## Burn Down the Town: The 1884 Flats Lumber Fires

Cleveland's most serious fire? Well, probably the East Ohio Gas Company fire, if you're talking corpses and ruined lives. At 130, its death toll edges out the Cleveland Clinic fire by at least five—and only quibblers would insist on the Collinwood School fire, which after all occurred outside Cleveland proper.

It's harder to make a choice if you're measuring property damage or a threat to the survival of the city. The 1883 Standard Oil fire (above) came within minutes and one jammed culvert of burning its way right up both sides of the Cuyahoga River all the way to the lakefront. The 1914 Fisher-Wilson lumber fire, too, threatened to consume at least the entire Flats in flames and even managed to *melt* away 300 feet of the Central Viaduct. My vote, though, would be for the twin 1884 Flats lumber fires, which not only threatened to burn down the whole city but were probably intended to accomplish just that.

Extending south along the Cuyahoga River from Whiskey Island, the Flats consists roughly of five peninsulas whose bulging projections sometimes leave persons on the east bank standing west of those actually standing on the river's west bank. In 1884, most of the third peninsula, including parts of Carter, Scranton, Girard, and Collins streets, and the CCC & I railroad tracks, was home to many of Cleveland's enormous lumberyards. This had been the case for some years. In February 1883, these yards had suffered terrible damage and losses when catastrophic floods had washed up to 25 million feet of lumber out into Lake Erie.

And then, in September 1884 someone decided to burn them down.

The initial arson was apparently committed in the Woods, Perry & Company lumberyards. Just before 7:00 p.m. on September 7, Frank Stepanek, a watchman for the Variety Iron Works, noticed a fire in a pile of shavings there and called in an alarm from Box 23. Chief James W. Dickinson got there within minutes with Engine Companies 1, 2, and 8 and Hook and Ladder Company No. 1, and he immediately called in four more companies and another hook-and-ladder unit. Cleveland's greatest fire was on.

For the first several hours it was no contest. With enormous lumber piles as high as 60 feet spread about in all directions and separated by narrow alleys that let in even more oxygen, the fire remorselessly advanced in all directions against the outmatched firemen and toward more waiting wood. Soon, the lumberyards and shops of the C. G. King Company, Potter, Birdsall and Company, Davidson and Howe, and the Novelty and Variety ironworks were enveloped in flames and smoke. The incredible heat generated by the burning of millions of board feet soon generated whirlwinds—mini-firestorms, really—that began to rain burning brands and sparks over downtown Cleveland, and even as far as East Cleveland. And as flames continued to blaze in a 15-to-20-acre triangle—1,100 by 1,300 by 1,300 feet—the fire jumped north across the river at about 10:00 p.m. and enveloped the Stanley Lard Oil and Candle Works, the Sherwin Williams Company, and the NYP & O freight depot. By now, 2,000 feet of river docking was also well on its way to becoming smouldering ashes. As the fire reached its climax late on the night of September 7, a Cleveland policeman watching it turned to his companion and said, "Go and repent! There's as good a picture of hell as you can get on this earth!"

Within two hours, the situation had escalated into the most serious threat in the city's history to its very survival. Virtually all fire units were now committed to the Flats inferno, leaving the rest of the city defenseless from further arson or accidental fires. Even as his wearying men continued their fighting retreat from the ever-growing flames, Chief Dickinson appealed for help to neighboring communities. And his plea was generously answered: before the crisis was over, firefighters and equipment from many communities were rushed to Cleveland. Help came from Painesville, Columbus, Elyria, Youngstown, Sandusky, Akron, Lorain, Toledo, Ashtabula, Delaware, Norwalk, Oberlin, Clyde, Galion, Fremont, and from Erie, Pennsylvania. The train carrying the engines from Painesville made the 30-mile trip in 28 minutes; the engineer of the Youngstown fire train didn't even set his brake. As an added precaution, the Fifth Regiment was called out at the Armory. Its purpose was to help prevent looting, if necessary, but it ended up dispersing lumber piles in the path of the advancing flames.

It was a miracle the fire was contained mostly in the Flats. (One reason it may not have burned north all the way to Lake Erie was the proverbial "lake effect"; the heated Flats helped create southerly winds that pushed the flames away from the lake.) With hundreds of burning brands and sparks broadcast for miles over the city, many persons spent sleepless nights beating out flames as fiery debris came down on Cleveland by the light of a full moon. Sparks were reported "thick as snow" on Prospect Avenue, and the ghastly light from the Flats could be seen as far away as Hudson, Akron, Wellington, Oberlin, Shelby, and just about everywhere within a 75-mile radius. The roof of the Handyside flour store on Ontario Street was set afire four times by sparks, and a two-story house on Wason Street burned down because there were no firemen available to put out the fire.

How hot was it? Well, workers cleaning up the wreckage later found kegs of nails completely melted together, barrels of broken glass fragments fused into one mass, and several tons of wood completely converted to coal that night. And the heat could be felt as far away as the upper windows of buildings on the eastern blocks of Superior Avenue.

As the long hours of September 7 gave way to September 8, the tide began to turn. The Cleveland fire forces couldn't do much to stop the holocaust in the Woods, Perry & Company area, but they succeeded admirably in preventing or putting out fires outside the critical region. The force's efforts were hobbled by a lack of adequate manpower—the entire force was only 150 men—and equipment. Access to the primary blaze was hindered by lack of a fireboat, and there was no firehouse in the area—despite Chief Dickinson's frequent prior pleas for both. And there is even some question as to the quality of the water supply: much of the water used on the fire was pumped directly from the river and was reputed to be so contaminated with grease and oil—probably from the Standard Oil works upstream, via Kingsbury Run—that firemen weren't sure whether their streams were aggravating the fire or putting it out. Anyway, much of the water available had to be sprayed directly on the firefighters to prevent the intense heat from overcoming them or setting their clothes on fire. Two engines, trapped by the enveloping flames, were pushed into the river by escaping firefighters.

As with most Cleveland disasters, the work of the safety forces was complicated and imperiled by the actions of the thousands of Clevelanders—acutely described by the *Cleveland Leader* as "adventurous loafers"—who came out to gape at the fiery, magnificent spectacle. One of them, at least, got his comeuppance. A male onlooker, apparently unaware that a nearby engine was pumping water directly from the Cuyahoga River, was seen greedily drinking with cupped hands from the spraying leak in a firehose. Minutes later, the same man was seen vomiting uncontrollably in the streets of Cleveland. The more fortunate qualities of Cleveland's populace were demonstarted by the dozens of old-time volunteer firemen from Cleveland's past who turned out unasked and unpaid to work side by side with their professional brethren. Another bright aspect was the report of a brigade of "motherly-appearing ladies bearing sandwiches and coffee for the firemen" who appeared in the Flats during that long night. It is said that Cleveland saloons did a roaring business all through the night and morning. One of them belonged to William Droge. Although his Canal Street saloon was in the path of the flames, he sold beer and whiskey even as a family at the rear of his building evacuated their belongings. He sold his last beer at 9:30 p.m. and announced with satisfaction, "Well, if this place goes up I won't have to move anything, as I am completely sold out."

When the morning of September 8 came the fire was under control. Over a million dollars of damage had been done, mostly to Flats lumber concerns, but also to CCC & I railroad tracks and rolling stock and Western Union lines and buildings. The main area of destruction probably took up 20 acres and as much as 50 million board feet of wood.

Unbelievably, there were no fatalities. A fireman named Dewey broke his ankle and Assistant Chief Rebbeck was knocked unconscious by falling lumber, which also smashed the foot of Frank Jennett of Engine Company No. 3 and the kneecap of No. 9's George Hemrich, and knocked out Jacob Beilier of No. 12. Many of the firemen were badly blistered by the heat: Chief Dickinson's face was said to look "like a bladder," while Assistant Chief George A. Wallace (Dickinson's future successor and Cleveland's most legendary fireman) "seems to have been boiled in wax, judging from his complexion, and his voice is *non est*."

Chief Dickinson was angry in the wake of the fire, especially as his recommendations after the Standard Oil Fire of the previous year had gone largely unheeded:

> I say now what I said after the Standard Oil fire, and that is that this city don't know what to expect in the direction of fires. It might have been worse than it was. We are liable to just such conflagrations at any time. Suppose that another destructive fire had broken out in the center of the city, what could we have done? My object in obtaining aid from outside was more to be prepared for such an emergency than anything else. Do you know that three of those companies coming in here had more men than we have in the whole department?

For obvious reasons, arsonists love Sundays. Exactly two weeks later, another fire broke out in the fifth peninsula of the Flats (the present-day Tremont area). Shortly before 11:00 a.m., the watchman at Monroe Brothers & Company discovered a fire in the center of its lumberyard. He immediately turned in an alarm from Box 57 at the corner of Jefferson Street and Centralway, but the fire was well under way by the time firemen arrived. It was brought under control three hours later, but another fire—also deliberately set—sprang up in the Monroe dry house over 300 feet away. As firemen rushed to extinguish it, yet another blaze erupted nearby at the Browne & Strong yard. Chief Dickinson knew the routine by now, and calls for help went out to Columbus, Painesville, Delaware, Galion, Toledo, Bellevue, Clyde, Oberlin, Elyria, Painesville, Ashtabula, and Akron.

It was another close call, but exhausted firefighters finally got the fire under control by 8:00 p.m. By then it had consumed property, mainly stacks of lumber, in a two-block area running over 1,100 feet from east to west, six acres in all. The fire's last gasp was yet another arson blaze discovered at 6:50 p.m. at the Bell, Cartright lumberyard. The accelerant used was probably coal oil. The fire drew another estimated 50,000 spectators, many of whom improved the economy of the local saloons.

Neither of the catastrophic 1884 Flats lumberyard arson fires was ever solved. Tramps or mischievous boys were the most likely suspects, and rumors that impending wage cuts had prompted both the Woods, Perry and Monroe Brothers arsons were angrily discounted by officials of both companies. It is also possible that both fires were started by sparks from either a passing river tugboat or one of the many locomotives passing through the area.

It was rumored during the Monroe Brothers blaze that a "slouchy-looking man" was overheard to say, "There'll be another fire here pretty soon," a prophecy soon fulfilled in the Monroe dry house and elsewhere. Several hours later, a suspect was arrested in the vicinity of the fire by Patrolman McMasters and apparently interrogated during the following week to no avail. He boasted the improbable name of Christ Schweitzer and was reported by the newspapers to be a "dissolute person well known by the police." Schweitzer was very nearly lynched by the crowd that had come out to gawk and interfere with the safety forces. To add insult to injury, the *Cleveland Press* further defamed him as "a man who some time ago chopped off one of his hands so that he would not be obliged to work and support his family." Nineteenth-century Clevelanders, like their 20th-century counterparts, apparently loathed arsonists, but they had it in for welfare cheats, too.

## The Ultimate Fire: The 1914 Fisher-Wilson Inferno

Most catastrophic fires come without telltale warning signs. So it was with Cleveland's last city-threatening conflagration, the 1914 Flats lumber fire. Indeed, just three hours before it broke out, Cleveland Fire Department assistant chief Charles B. Whyler stated publicly, albeit injudiciously: "Cleveland's clean-up [of hazardous fire conditions] will decrease fire loss 50 per cent." Alas, his boast was not to be.

Whyler should have known and probably did know better. Although Cleveland fire losses were well below the national average, underlying conditions suggested an unwholesome fire profile for the Forest City. There were known water-pressure problems in the Flats area—the city's industrial core—and the 1912 National Underwriters' Report had severely criticized the shortcomings of Cleveland's fire department: "[It] is below the average, and the city [is] severely criticized as having a weak distribution system for its water supply and needing a higher pressure service."

The Flats were really just an accident waiting to happen. That accident happened on May 25, 1914.

It began in the extensive Fisher-Wilson lumberyards, adjacent to the Central Viaduct and the Nickel Plate trestle spanning the Cuyahoga River, near West Third and Stone's Levee. No one will ever really know how it started, but it was clearly arson. Cleveland authorities later flirted without result with the notions that mischievous boys threw matches into sawdust or that tramps hurled lit cigarettes into piles of wood shavings strewn carelessly about the Fisher-Wilson yards.

Whatever the cause, the blaze was first spotted at 8:30 p.m. by Engineer Frank Kaftan from his perch atop the "Big Four" railroad bridge near the Fisher-Wilson lot. He ran to end of the bridge and called in the alarm. It was already too late, as he subsequently recalled: "It was just a small blaze when I saw it first. But by the time I had turned in an alarm from tower KD at the end of the bridge it looked to be out of control."

And so it was: even as the words "North One!" went out to the fire department—indicating the origin of the fire—Cleveland's greatest 20th-century fire was well on its way to burning down the entire city.

It was almost as if the Fates had conspired to create a perfect nightmare for the Cleveland Fire Department. Thanks to the congestion caused by railroad locomotives and rolling stock in the Flats, firemen found their access to the fire hampered and even blocked altogether for precious minutes at key points. And though fireboats were already steaming up the Cuyahoga to fight the flames, firemen

Fisher, Wilson & Company advertisement, 1890s.

on the scene battled inadequate water pressure, lack of coal to fuel their engines, wildly erratic winds, and ever-increasing heat. For at least three hours flames raged unchecked north and south of the Central Viaduct, consuming everything in their path, driving firemen ever backward, and raising fears that they would obliterate the entire city by morning. After burning up about four million feet of hardwood at Fisher-Wilson, the flames moved into the millions of board feet at the Martin-Barriss lumberyards. Unsatisfied, the fire next reached for the enormous Saginaw Bay lumberyards, the Nickel Plate trestle, and the Central Viaduct.

As midnight neared, the fate of the city seemed dire. By now, a half-square-mile area of the Flats was in flames or ashes, and burning embers, cast by strong winds, were creating incendiary havoc as far away as East 40th Street. A six-story elevator of the Cleveland Grain Company was now afire, an adjacent nine-story elevator was threatened, and fire engines in the zone of maximum danger were shutting down for lack of available fuel. It must have seemed like a lost cause to Chief George A. Wallace and his beleaguered force of 225 Cleveland firemen, all of whom were in the Flats that night.

Somehow, at about midnight, the tide turned. This was partly due to sheer heroism on the part of Cleveland firemen: fighting with watery blasts from every vantage point—especially from perilous stations atop the flame-enveloped Central Viaduct and Nickel Plate trestle—they managed to prevent the fire from spreading beyond its lumberyard feeding grounds. At a critical juncture, the coaling ship *Pittsburgh* managed to steam up the Cuyahoga River with crucial fuel for the fire engines. More importantly, as Assistant Chief Whyler later admitted, the issue was decided by a change in the wind. About midnight, it shifted abruptly—and pushed the flames back toward their origin, thoroughly burning out whatever they had missed in the Fisher-Wilson and Martin-Barriss lumberyards. The fire was virtually under control by 2:30 a.m. and was officially declared so at 9:00 a.m. on May 26. Chief Wallace stepped down his force on the scene from 30 companies to 20 at 8:00 a.m., and then down to ten companies at noon.

By that time the fire had long since done its worst. Although firemen on both spans fought fiercely, both the Nickel Plate and Central Viaduct bridges were casualties of the blaze. About 350 feet of the Central Viaduct literally melted from the heat of the lumber fires below, and the fall of its fiery debris collapsed at least 200 feet of the Nickel Plate trestle below.

Clevelanders awoke to a smoking ruin at the center of their city on May 26, 1914. Up to 20 million feet of Flats lumber lay burning or in ashes. A good part of the Flats was covered with half a foot of the water Cleveland firemen had aimed at the flames. And one of Cleveland's main thoroughfares—the Central Viaduct—was ruined, as was one of its vital railroad arteries, the Nickel Plate crossing over the Flats. The Viaduct damage would have been worse had not Chief Wallace supervised the removal of much of its oil-soaked planking.

All in all, the Viaduct inferno furnished the most dramatic moments of the catastrophe. Despite the efforts of frantic firemen and repeated charges by Cleveland police, thousands of eager spectators thronged the south end of the Central Viaduct. Most of them

Photograph of burnt Central Viaduct. *Cleveland Press,* May 26, 1914.

would not leave even as the flames licked hungrily at their feet. The reward for their persistence eventually came when a crazed man broke through police lines at West 14th and ran toward the already collapsing Viaduct. He reached the core of the flames, recoiled from the burning metal of the bridge rail—and jumped over the side into the hot core of the Flats lumber fire. It was the only fatality of the 1914 Flats fire.

It could have been worse. The Ringling Brothers Circus was in town that fatal night, and, believe it or not, had pitched its big top in the Flats. Shortly after 8:30 p.m. several frightened men ran past the entrance of the filled tent crying "Fire!" It is recorded that shrewd, burly circus personnel instantly seized the criers and beat them into immediate silence with tent pins, fists, and whatever else lay at hand. Thereupon, the ringmaster calmly informed the audience that the circus was adjourning a half hour early—and admonished them to file out in order. They did, and Cleveland was spared an additional catastrophe of mass disorder to sully an already unfortunate night. Potential panic among the circus folk was averted by the soothing mien of Georgia Hartzell, the wardrobe mistress and unofficial "Mother" to the many young and unmarried females of the troupe. She moved among her charges, dispensing reassurance, even as 25 circus cars—worth $30,000—burned up in the night. Upcoming shows in Marion and Toledo were canceled, but new trains were already speeding westward to put the circus back on its feet and on the road.

Other than the unidentified suicide, no civilians or firemen were badly injured. But the disaster did not lack for terrible moments or heroic acts. Lieutenant Dittman of Engine Company No. 2 and six of his men were overcome by fire and smoke while fighting flames at an oil shed owned by the Big Four Railroad; they escaped, but Dittman was carried away unconscious. And tragedy was narrowly averted by the men of Hook and Ladder Company No. 6 and other firefighters as the fire reached its climax about midnight. Trapped by flames on all sides while up on the Central Viaduct, they made a desperate dash right through a wall of flames to safety on the east side. And firemen were not the only heroes that memorable night. Frank G. Hogen and W. H. Gray organized a battalion of 50 school custodians who manned a bucket brigade to keep the East 14th-Central Avenue neighborhood from being torched by the numberless embers and burning brands cast into the air by the inferno. Hogen and his men put out at least 12 fires that night. And T. W. Cannell, the superintendent of the city garbage department, labored successfully with several dozen of his men to save the department's Flats stables—and their 150 horses—from the hungry fires.

As always, the fire also kindled less heroic behavior. Many tramps, rousted by the fire from their customary haunts in Flats lumber piles, groggily stumbled forward to beg or steal food and coffee intended for the firemen. Pickpockets, deprived of expected prey at the circus by its abrupt end, sauntered forth to find victims among the estimated 250,000 Clevelanders who came out to see the Flats burn down. A man named John Gladish was robbed and severely beaten by three men, while unlucky Charles Kammin was robbed and stabbed, probably by the same gang. Most Clevelanders present, however, behaved themselves by not getting in the way of the firemen any more than usual.

The final bill for damages totaled somewhere between a million and a one and a half million dollars. Because the costly damage to both the Viaduct and the Nickel Plate trestle was due to the immense piles of lumber stored *right underneath* them, irate acting Cleveland mayor John N. Stockwell loudly demanded legislation to prevent such conditions from occurring again. The Viaduct and the Nickel Plate were quickly repaired, and the city put its last truly life-threatening fire behind it.

# SMITHEREEN STREET

## The West 117th Street Explosion

## (1953)

All Cleveland disasters are not created equal. Especially, it would seem, if they happen on the West Side. You don't believe it? Consider, then, the 1953 West 117th Street disaster. In just a few seconds of unexpected violence it destroyed an entire mile of a heavily industrialized Cleveland thoroughfare. It killed one person and put 64 more in hospitals. The force of its explosions catapulted at least a dozen cars high above the street, along with their stunned occupants. It lifted hundreds of huge concrete slabs into the air and then rained them down on terrified motorists and pedestrians. It bounced 100 weighty manhole covers into the sky, whence they descended to penetrate vulnerable homes and apartments. It smithereened 5,000 feet of road, damaged and disrupted two railroads and a trolley line, not to mention pulverizing the water, sewer, and gas infrastructure along the border of two cities. It caused $5 million in damage and stimulated half that amount again in lawsuits. And the odds are that, if you don't hail from the West Side, you've never heard of it.

It was the height of the Cleveland rush hour and the traffic light at West 117th and Madison was about to turn red when the first blast came at exactly 5:15 p.m. on September 10. Investigators later pinpointed its genesis at the intersection of Detroit Avenue and West 117th. Owing to the nature of the explosion, however, the upheaval

West 117th Street at the New York Central railroad tracks, epicenter of the explosion.

from the blast instantaneously transmitted itself both north and south on West 117th via the six-foot sanitary sewer that ran along the western edge between Lake Avenue and Berea Road. Finding additional fuel as it raced through the disintegrating sewer, the blast reached the peak of its destruction at the intersections of West 117th Street with Berea Road, Madison Avenue, and Lake Avenue. The first and most obvious result was that much of the surface of West 117th was suddenly thrust upward several feet with incredible force, trampolining at least a dozen cars into the air. The second, and more lethal, effect was the shattering of the adjacent sidewalks and retaining walls, especially in the area by the New York Central Railroad overpass (the current site of the West 117th Street RTA station). What goes up must come down, and even as the first automobiles crashed to the street, airborne concrete chunks—some of them as large as 20 feet by 10 feet—began to descend. For those unlucky humans on the scene, it became an instant hell on earth.

Charles Flickinger's experience was typical for motorists in the area. Waiting for the light at Clifton Boulevard and West 117th, he heard a "sudden bang." The next thing he knew, he was lying in the street, looking at his car smashed into a bus. Worse yet was the ordeal of Robert Hudson. He heard "a big explosion and saw a pink flash," the pyrotechnic prelude to having his car thrown 15 feet into the air, where it collided with another auto and then crashed down. And there were several drivers who shared the fate of Herman Heppner, who remembered it this way: "I heard an explosion and everything went black. The next thing I knew my car was upside down on top of another car and four men were chopping my windshield to get out."

It could have been worse—and it was for Katherine Szabo, 42, and Eleanor Rinaldi, 24. Katherine, driving in a borrowed car with her brother Robert, had just cleared the New York Central overpass when the street exploded. Her car, at the epicenter of the catastrophe, was one of the first hurled into the air and probably the first to be crushed by the concrete fallout from the blast. Seconds later, the car caught on fire. Robert managed to crawl out of the wreckage and the fire was soon extinguished. But Katherine didn't make it, dying of her injuries shortly after she was taken to St. John's Hospital. Amazingly, she was the only fatality of the rush-hour disaster. But Eleanor Rinaldi came close to joining her in death. She was motoring with her husband, Angelo, when the first blast caught them by the overpass, and she was trapped when a huge concrete slab smashed through the car roof and crushed the dashboard area into her legs. While firemen desperately labored to extricate her smashed body, Father James O'Brien, a priest from the nearby Sts. Philip and James parish, consoled the still-conscious Rinaldi and administered the last rites of the Roman Catholic Church to her. Astonishingly, Rinaldi survived her ordeal and could not remember anything after her car cleared the underpass.

Things weren't much better for the hapless pedestrians in the five-block explosion area. Margaret Calvey was waiting for the bus at Berea Road when "the ground shook and the sidewalk rose up and struck me in the face. I was blown right out of my shoes." Joy Moore was leaning against a delicatessen window when she heard the first blast and then watched in stupefied horror as a rain of bricks, pavement, and streetcar tracks began to fall around her. One of the most seriously injured was Joyce Bauer, 22, who was standing with two other women in front of the Glidden Company plant at West 117th and Berea Road when the street detonated. Caught in the sudden shower of concrete and miscellaneous debris, she finished her day in critical condition at Lakewood Hospital.

Among those who endured a different kind of fright were Sue Townsend of 1497 West 117th and Edwin Hood of 11708 Detroit Avenue. As they abruptly learned, the force of the multiple explosions had sent 100 heavy metal manhole covers temporarily skyward. Townsend was preparing dinner in her second-floor flat when she heard a noise like an auto crash. As she ran to the window, a manhole cover came through the kitchen ceiling and smashed halfway through the floor. About the same moment, another bored through the top of Hood's fourth-floor apartment, took off his living room door, and drilled into an unoccupied third-floor apartment.

There were at least four explosions in all, although the worst of the violence and damage was wrought within the first few seconds at 5:15 p.m. Within minutes, safety forces poured into the stricken area. Much of the locale was flooded by broken water mains pouring millions of gallons into the ruins, a torrent that threatened to aggravate the public health peril of the wrecked sanitary sewer system. East Ohio workers began capping gas lines exposed by the blasts, and Red Cross workers began distributing water and sandwiches. Indeed, for the most part, the disaster spectacle over the next 48 hours was a showcase of Cleveland at its finest, with the terrors and challenges of the tragedy bringing out the best in all. All except, naturally, the crowds of thousands of unappeasable spectators, who continually impeded safety forces. After touring the ruins, Mayor Thomas Burke, in high dudgeon, vented civic spleen: "I was disgusted when I saw men and women taking little children into the explosion area. It was undoubtedly thoughtlessness on their part but they blocked rescue work."

Ground Zero on Smithereen Street: West 117th Street at the New York Central railroad bridge.

Within a week, the sewers were rebuilt, roadway repairs were under way, and most of the victims had left the hospital. The cities of Cleveland and Lakewood, which shared the West 117th Street boundary, were now free to concentrate on discovering what exactly had occurred there. As is typical of Cleveland disasters, they didn't succeed very well.

It wasn't for lack of resources or expertise. Coroner Sam Gerber was put in charge of the official probe, and he immediately recruited Dr. George W. Barnes, Dr. Leon W. Weinberger, and Professor George Blum from Case Institute of Technology. These appointments augured well, especially as Barnes had headed the probe into the 1944 East Ohio Gas Company fire, and the team enjoyed additional resources provided by experts from the U.S. Bureau of Mines. But the formal report of the Gerber team, issued in March 1954, failed to answer the question of exactly who and what were responsible for the disaster. Ruling out escaping natural gas (either from East Ohio lines or the numerous abandoned gas wells that dotted—and still dot—the West 117th area) or sewer gas

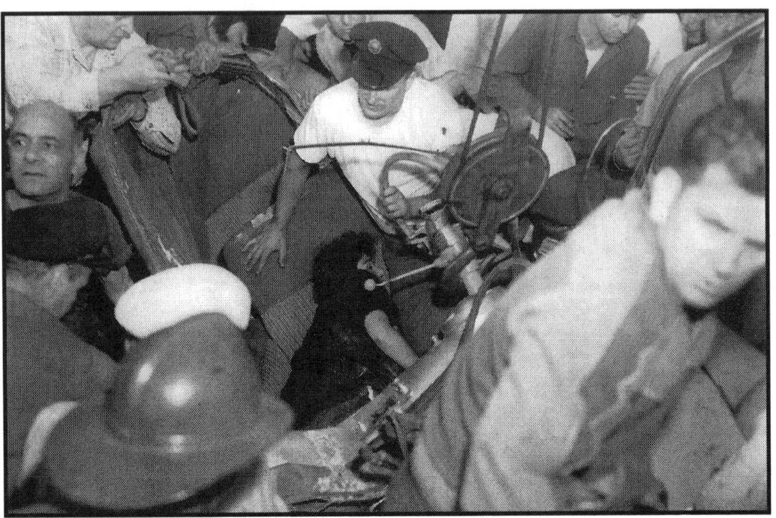

From out of the jaws of death: safety forces try to extricate Eleanor Rinaldi from her car, September 10, 1953.

(which had caused two East Side explosions just previous to the West 117th blast), Gerber's probers focused on the evidence of flammable industrial waste and gasoline found in the shattered sanitary sewer lines. Their conclusion was that area plants had been illegally dumping such hazardous wastes for some time before they ignited on September 10, 1953. What had pushed them to critical mass was a hot, dry summer, which curtailed the normal flushing action of the sewers. By September 10, it was just a disaster waiting to happen. In all probability, a chance friction spark or a carelessly thrown cigarette had triggered the initial explosion. Gerber's report further noted that there were 194 area plants using flammable substances, but it refused to speculate on the exact origins of whatever blew up five blocks of city street.

The last word about the tragedy, inevitably, belonged to the lawyers. Gerber & Co. may have embraced a masterly ambiguity about the source of the explosions, but the lawyers who brought the 91 personal injury lawsuits filed were uninterested in such coyness. Lawyers for injured plaintiffs brought suits totaling $2.5 million

Automobile crushed by flying concrete near the New York Central Railroad overpass, September 10, 1953.

against Sun Oil, Shell Oil, White Sewing Machine, Union Carbide, Ferbert-Schorndorfer, and the cities of Cleveland and Lakewood. The five firms were accused of dumping flammable substances that caused the disaster, and the cities were held liable for permitting such illegal practices. In the end, however, four years later, the plaintiffs got little for their troubles. Under the persuasive aegis of Common Pleas Court judge William K. Thomas, attorneys reached an out-of-court settlement in June of 1957. With both cities agreeing to pay a third apiece and the five firms dividing the last third of the payment, the victims settled for a total of $205,000. One of the smallest amounts, $3,000, went to Julius Szabo, who had suffered the greatest loss of all, his wife Katherine. No fault whatsoever was admitted by any defendant. And so ended one of the West Side's worst, and undeservedly obscure, disasters. Let us hope that the present guardians of our public safety are more alert than those caught snoozing on September 10, 1953.

# PHOTO CREDITS

Photographs and illustrations are from the *Cleveland Press* Collection, Cleveland State University Archives, except:

Page 43, author's collection; p. 47, *Plain Dealer*; p. 51, Western Reserve Historical Society; p. 59–63, *Cleveland Press*; p. 67–81, *Cleveland News*; p. 83, *Cleveland Press*; p. 89, Cleveland Public Library; p. 97, Cleveland Clinic Foundation Archives; p. 100, Cleveland Public Library; p. 111–113, *Cleveland Press*; p. 116, *Plain Dealer*; p. 117, *Cleveland Leader*; p. 118–121, *Cleveland Press*; p. 125, Author's Collection; p. 126, *Cleveland News*; p. 128, *Cleveland Press*; p. 136, *Cleveland News*; p. 143, *Plain Dealer*; p. 147–149, Cleveland Public Library; p. 150, *Cleveland Press*; p. 153–155, *Plain Dealer*; p. 161, *Cleveland Press*; p. 169–173, Cleveland Public Library; p. 179, *Cleveland World*; p. 181, *Cleveland Press*; p. 184–185, *Cleveland Leader*; p. 188, Cleveland Police Historical Society; p. 194, author's collection; p. 195–199, *Cleveland Press*; p. 209, author's collection; p. 211, *Cleveland Press*.

# More True Crime & Disaster Tales . . .

## They Died Crawling

And Other Tales of Cleveland Woe

John Stark Bellamy II

The foulest crimes and worst disasters in Cleveland history are recounted in 15 incredible-but-true tales. Delves into the city's most notorious moments, from the 1916 waterworks collapse to the Cleveland Clinic fire to the sensational Sam Sheppard murder trial. These gripping narratives deliver high drama and dark comedy, heroes and villains.

*"A rollicking, no-holds-barred account of the facts (and continued speculation) about some of the darkest events and weirdest people in Cleveland's history." – Youngstown Vindicator*

## The Maniac in the Bushes

More Tales of Cleveland Woe

John Stark Bellamy II

Thirteen more incredible true stories of Cleveland crime and disaster from the author of "They Died Crawling." Meet Martha Wise, the Merry Widow of Medina, who poisoned relatives because she enjoyed funerals; Cleveland Safety Director Eliot Ness and his nemesis, the "Mad Butcher of Kingsbury Run"; and many other local heroes and villains.

*"Morbidly fascinating and wickedly entertaining." —The Plain Dealer*

## The Corpse in the Cellar

And Further Tales of Cleveland Woe

John Stark Bellamy II

The third book in Bellamy's popular series delivers 25 more true stories of Cleveland crime and disaster. Includes crotchety vigilante Jarvis Meach, who shot down robbers in cold blood; wicked stepmother Mary Garrett, who locked her stepdaughters in their bedroom and set fire to the house; the great Ashtabula bridge disaster; and more.

*"Bellamy writes with razor-edged wit and his own particular brand of charm." —Medina County Gazette*

More at **www.grayco.com**

## More True Crime & Disaster Tales . . .

### The Killer in the Attic

And More True Tales of Crime and Disaster from Cleveland's Past

John Stark Bellamy II

This fourth collection of Cleveland crime and disaster features 26 more gruesome, horrible, tragic—and true—tales. Includes Mafia legend Shondor Birns, whose high-profile life of crime came to an explosive end in his Lincoln Continental, and two doomed workmen buried alive in the very concrete that became a Cleveland landmark, the Terminal Tower.

*"Fascinating and yes entertaining . . . often in a bizarre way that leaves the reader feeling guilty for being so entertained." —Medina County Gazette*

### Death Ride at Euclid Beach

And Other True Tales of Crime & Disaster from Cleveland's Past

John Stark Bellamy II

#5 in Bellamy's popular series delivers 26 more tales of Cleveland crimes and disasters. Includes one of Cleveland's most baffling murder mysteries: the brutal murder of 16-year-old Beverly Jarosz in her suburban bedroom. Bellamy's stories are meticulously researched and delivered in a literate and entertaining style.

*"Has more than its fair share of violence, sex, debauchery and reversals of fortune . . . But what emerges between the lines are stories of human suffering, stories of class struggle, stories that speak as much to the criminal mind as to the crime itself." – Sun Newspapers*

### The Last Days of Cleveland

and More True Tales of Crime and Disaster from Cleveland's Past

John Stark Bellamy II

#6 in this Cleveland crime and disaster series. These 15 stories are sometimes gruesome, often surprising, meticulously researched and delivered in a literate and entertaining style. Meet a daring Jazz Age stick-up man, a murderous grandmother, an ageless fire chief addicted to profanity, and other unforgettable characters.

*"Heroes and rogues fill the pages of this book. The stories will hold your attention and chill you to the bone." —Crime Shadow News*

More at **www.grayco.com**

# More True Crime & Disaster Tales . . .

## Women Behaving Badly

True Tales of Cleveland's Most Ferocious Female Killers: An Anthology

John Stark Bellamy II

A book for women with a wicked side! Why are women who murder so much more fascinating than their male counterparts? For evidence of that tantalizing truth, dip into this strange-but-true anthology by Cleveland's top historical crime writer. These 16 tales of willful women and their woeful misdeeds make for awfully entertaining reading.

*"Bellamy once again masterfully brings to life decades-old tales that won't let you look away." – Cleveland Magazine*

## Ten Ohio Disasters

Stories of Tragedy and Courage that Should Not Be Forgotten

Neil Zurcher

Ten disasters from Ohio's past deliver tragic lessons and inspiring examples of heroism. Revisit the devastating Xenia tornado, the sudden and shocking Silver Bridge collapse, the statewide Blizzard of '78, the deadly Who concert stampede in Cincinnati, an ill-fated group parachute jump over Lake Erie, the Fitchville nursing home fire, and others.

## Amy: My Search for Her Killer

Secrets and Suspects in the Unsolved Murder of Amy Mihaljevic

James Renner

A young journalist investigates the cold case that has haunted him since childhood: the 1989 disappearance of 10-year-old Amy Mihaljevic from Bay Village, Ohio. Filled with mysterious riddles, incredible coincidences, and a cast of odd but very real characters, his investigation quickly becomes a riveting journey in search of the truth.

*"Poignant and wonderfully well-written." – Richard North Patterson, New York Times bestselling author of Silent Witness*

More at **www.grayco.com**

# More True Crime & Disaster Tales . . .

## The Serial Killer's Apprentice

And Other True Stories of Cleveland's Most Intriguing Unsolved Crimes

James Renner

An investigative journalist cracks open Northeast Ohio's most intriguing unsolved crimes, including the 1964 murder of Garfield Heights teen Beverly Jarosz; the mysterious suicide (or murder?) of Joseph Kupchik; Ted Conrad and Cleveland's strangest bank heist; and other equally haunting tales.

*"James Renner is genuine. He cares about these victims . . . When it comes to true crime, this is the kind of writer we need." – Crime Shadow News*

## Cleveland Cops

The Real Stories They Tell Each Other

John H. Tidyman

Gritty, hilarious, and heartbreaking, these remarkable true stories take you on the roller coaster ride that is life as a Cleveland police officer. Listen in on stories the rest of us rarely get to hear: The biggest arrests, dumbest criminals, funniest practical jokes, and scariest moments. It's an inside look at the toughest job in town.

*"This book should be required reading for every elected official and for every citizen." – Chief Edward P. Kovacic (retired), Cleveland Police Department*

## Punched, Kicked, Spat On, and Sometimes Thanked

Memoirs of a Cleveland TV News Reporter

Paul Orlousky

A veteran Cleveland TV reporter shares backstories behind the news stories he covered over 50 years: historic events, horrific crimes, bizarre behavior, heartwarming deeds, and some hilarious, silly stuff. "Orlo" earned his reputation for aggressive reporting—getting threats, punches, and kicks from investigation subjects but thanks from viewers.

More at **www.grayco.com**